I0140873

Bahá'í Public Speaking

**Teacher's Guide with Nine Workshops
for Children, Youth and Adults**

Dr. Randie S. Gottlieb

UnityWorks LLC

Bahá'í Public Speaking

ISBN: 978-0-9828979-8-0

© 2014 UnityWorks LLC
First edition 2001, second edition 2007

<u>All rights reserved</u>. No part of this book may be reproduced or transmitted in any form or by any means without prior written permission from the publisher.

<u>Handouts</u>: UnityWorks hereby grants permission to the purchaser to copy the handouts as needed for their students. The copyright information must clearly show on all copies. Scanning, large-scale reproduction or distribution, and inclusion in commercial publications are not permitted.

<u>Bulk Purchase</u>: Please contact us with your request: info@UnityWorksStore.com.

<u>Disclaimer</u>: It is the responsibility of the user to determine the suitability of the materials and activities in this book, and the associated downloaded items, to meet the user's particular needs and the needs of the teachers, children or students involved. The user therefore agrees to hold the author and UnityWorks, along with its personnel, employees, agents, contractors or volunteers, harmless from any claims and/or litigation arising from or related thereto. Reasonable caution and adult supervision of children is recommended at all times.

If you find these items useful, please let others know about them.

Thank you!

www.UnityWorksStore.com

Special thanks to my husband, Steven E. Gottlieb, M.D. for his ongoing support.

Edited by Steven Gottlieb
Production assistance, Jordan Gottlieb

Quotations from the Bahá'í writings reprinted with permission of the National Spiritual Assembly of the Bahá'ís of the United States and the Bahá'í Publishing Trust of Wilmette, IL.

Clip art images taken or adapted from:
The Big Box of Art from www.Hemera.com

All websites and references listed are correct at the time of publication.

Published by UnityWorks, LLC
Yakima, Washington, USA

What People Are Saying

"Bahá'í Public Speaking is a treasure-trove of vital tools for the Bahá'í community! It is extremely well-written and thoughtfully organized. You are getting right at the heart of things—really working on the nuts and bolts of utterance, our main vehicle for getting the message of the Faith out of our hearts and into the hearts of others. Perhaps most important for me, it's all laid out and ready to go." —**Kellie Heath**

"Fabulous! I'm very glad that you're publishing this. I hope it is widely circulated!" —**Erica Toussaint**

"Very well presented, easy to read and follow, sensible, logical, helpful." —**Gerald Filson, Office of External Affairs, NSA of Canada**

"Totally delighted that you've done this; it is so important that EVERY believer feel themselves capable of presenting the Faith to others." —**Celia Merritt Johnson**

"Our final class is on Sunday. Twelve junior youth are doing it. It's gone wonderfully! The participants truly enjoyed their time and I saw marked improvement. The last day we had the parents come to watch a final presentation. This went over very well. This course offers participants a friendly and encouraging way to build confidence in speaking. A fantastic bonus to the class is watching young people learning how to look into the Holy Writings for answers to their questions. THANK YOU for putting this together." —**Sue Kutches**

"The manual should be a great help for all of us to improve our ability to present the Faith to the public!" —**Suzanne Henck, Hong Kong Bahá'í Institute**

"I just wanted to give you a quick update on the effectiveness of the public speaking curriculum. We are putting the activities into action as part of the Plan. I have asked the youth to take the initiative to host firesides, to invite friends and share their presentations as part of the expansion phases of the IPGs. This is indeed an exciting development!

"The youth have had to give presentations at their schools and their cluster reflection meetings, and they have gone REALLY well! Parents and others noticed a difference in their ability to present information clearly and effectively and mentioned how wonderful this was. It totally complements Ruhi. It's a way of adding confidence to the presentations. I think this is so practical." —**Juli Redson-Smith**

Dedicated to

Jonathan, Jordan & Steve

TABLE OF CONTENTS

INTRODUCTION

Bahá'u'lláh has ordained that "complete victory" of the Cause "should be achieved through speech and utterance."[1] "It is not desirable," He declares, "that a man be left without knowledge or skills, for he is then but a barren tree. Then, so much as capacity and capability allow, ye needs must deck the tree of being with fruits such as knowledge, wisdom, spiritual perception and eloquent speech."[2]

This teacher's guide is designed to prepare Bahá'ís of all ages to effectively share the Faith and its Sacred Writings with others "through speech and utterance." Participants will learn to speak clearly and with confidence at devotional gatherings, study circles, children's classes, firesides, home visits, Feasts and Holy Days, school presentations, public talks and other events. Local Assemblies will also find it to be a useful resource for seeker response representatives, media committees, public information officers, youth workshops and campus clubs.

Furthermore, 'Abdu'l-Bahá has instructed us to "encourage...the school children, from their earliest years, to deliver speeches of high quality."[3]

The Universal House of Justice has called upon us to involve Bahá'í children and youth in "programmes of activity that will engage their interests [and] mold their capacities for teaching and service."[4]

The International Teaching Centre has affirmed that "these young people should then be seen as a door to entry by troops and as a fruitful source of teachers ...not simply as children for whom activity must be arranged...but as a living creation of God necessary at this very moment for the purposes of God..."[5]

As our children and youth arise to play their part in contributing to the betterment of society, these public speaking workshops should help to confirm their Bahá'í identity, strengthen their reliance on God, and empower them to express with increasing eloquence "high ideals and goals" so they may "cast their beams like brilliant candles on the world."[6]

References:

1. Tablets of Bahá'u'lláh, p. 197
2. Bahá'u'lláh, Bahá'í Education: A Compilation. p.5
3. Selections from 'Abdu'l-Bahá, p. 134
4. Ridván 2000 Message
5. Letter to the Boards of Counselors, 5 Dec. 1988
6. Selections from 'Abdu'l-Bahá, p.136

Development of the Public Speaking Workshops

This public speaking workshop series grew out of direct needs in the field, in response to repeated requests from local Assemblies and their committees for believers who could speak clearly and competently about the Faith, whether offering a prayer at a devotional gathering, teaching a children's class, giving a fireside, sharing a Feast report, telling stories at a Holy Day celebration, presenting materials to public officials, speaking at a large event, or talking with a family around the kitchen table during a home visit. The workshops have been tested and refined in several countries over a period of about thirty years.

For example, in 1985, when Bahá'í communities were asked to present "The Promise of World Peace" to local officials, one Spiritual Assembly decided to train children and youth to make the presentation and to answer any questions that might arise. Practical, step-by-step lessons were developed and the young believers practiced until they were ready. Then, with complete confidence and poise, they presented copies of the document to the mayor and each member of the city council. Their gift was warmly received. The council meeting was televised that day, and the Bahá'í presentation was broadcast on the evening news to the entire community.

Over the years, workshop participants have suggested that these lessons should be compiled in a form that others could use, leading to the publication of "Bahá'í Public Speaking" in 2001. The book is written in plain language, so it can be used by older youth and adults with no formal training. It includes detailed lesson plans for nine two-hour workshops, with sample publicity materials, student handouts, evaluation forms, and a certificate of completion.

In addition to the exercises in public speaking, there are also sections on:

- **Tutoring Reading**
  Students practice reading the Bahá'í Writings with fluency and reverence, to capture more fully the spirit and beauty of the sacred Word. By learning effective techniques for tutoring reading, the teacher will also be able to provide this service in other settings.

- **Memorization Techniques**
  Bahá'u'lláh tells His followers to memorize passages from the heavenly scriptures "so that in the course of their speech they may recite divine verses whenever the occasion demandeth it…" *(Tablets of Bahá'u'lláh, p. 200)*

- **Approaching the Media** and **Responding to Controversy**
  As the Faith becomes more widely-known, Baha'is will need to develop skills in relating to local media outlets and in responding positively to public criticism or attacks on the Faith.

- **Additional Projects**
  Activities for younger children, ideas for dramatic presentations, and plans for a youth fireside are included.

Overview and Objectives

This easy-to-use teacher's guide on Bahá'í public speaking is designed to prepare children, youth and adults with the knowledge, spiritual insights and skills needed to more effectively serve the Faith.

The nine workshops are organized in a sequential format, each activity building on the previous one. Each lesson includes a warm-up, review questions, speaking tips, practice exercises, student handouts and a homework assignment.

In addition to developing spiritual insights, these workshops are designed to systematically increase confidence and skill through a hands-on approach with ample opportunity for practice and constructive feedback. Participants will learn to research the Bahá'í Writings, memorize selected passages, prepare and deliver brief talks on the Faith, and develop their speaking style.

Specific objectives are listed below.

Participants will learn to:

- Stand up with courage in front of a group

- Speak with a strong clear voice

- Use good posture and eye contact

- Read aloud well

- Memorize Bahá'í passages

- Answer questions about the Faith

- Research a topic from the Writings

- Write a speech

- Give a short prepared talk

- Give a short impromptu talk

- Introduce another speaker

- Present Bahá'í materials to local officials

- Speak through an interpreter

- Use a microphone

- Be interviewed by the media

GETTING STARTED

Sponsorship

When organizing the public speaking workshops, you may wish to ask a Local Spiritual Assembly or Bahá'í School to serve as the official sponsor. In addition to providing legal protection, that institution can help arrange opportunities for the students to practice what they have learned during and after the course.

The participants might be encouraged, for example, to recite a memorized quote at a devotional gathering, to speak at a fireside, to share a story with a children's class, or to serve as master of ceremonies for a Holy Day program.

The sponsor may also wish to prepare a short written message to the participants, encouraging them in their studies and commending their desire to be of service.

Facility

Classes can take place in a home, a Bahá'í Center, school or other suitable facility. There should be adequate parking and access to public transportation if necessary, kitchen and bathroom facilities, a classroom area, and space for students to practice their speeches without disturbing others.

Participants

The public speaking course has been designed particularly with youth and junior youth in mind, but it is also suitable for adults. Some of the lessons can be adapted to the needs of younger children. Bahá'ís and friends of the Faith can be invited.

Based on experience, the ideal class size is 8-10 students for each teacher. Smaller groups are workable but will not have the same dynamic. With a larger group, there will not be enough time for students to practice each skill in front of the class.

Teachers

One teacher should be recruited for each group of students. Teachers do not need to be professionally trained, but should possess certain qualities that are essential to the success of the class. They should be patient, encouraging, enthusiastic, reliable, organized, well-prepared, able to lead discussions and to demonstrate the various speaking skills.

Parents and youth can also be recruited to serve as assistants. With a little practice, they should be able to serve as teachers for public speaking workshops in the future. Teachers and any assistants should review the quotations on speech (Appendix A) before the workshop begins.

Class Schedule

The public speaking course consists of a series of nine workshops, each designed to build on the previous one. Each lesson is approximately two hours long. Sessions can be held weekly, monthly, or as often as desired. The entire workshop series can be offered during an intensive weekend retreat or summer school. The beginning lessons can also be divided up and used for children's activities during Feast, Unit Convention or cluster reflection meetings.

Between meeting times, students should practice with each other or with a mentor, either in person or over the phone. Students may learn best when the sessions are spaced out over time so there is ample opportunity to practice, perform, reflect, and grow into their new skills gradually and with confidence.

Materials

Participants should be asked to bring a notebook, pen and prayer book, but the teacher should also be ready to supply these materials if needed. In addition, it will helpful to have the following items available for each class:

- ☐ Easel and chalk board or white board with markers and eraser
- ☐ Basic Bahá'í pamphlets on a variety of topics
- ☐ Bahá'í books or computer programs for in-depth research
- ☐ Dictionary, thesaurus and 3x5 cards
- ☐ Stop watch or clock with a second hand
- ☐ Audio or video recorder
- ☐ Podium or small table
- ☐ Refreshments

PUBLICITY

Informing the Bahá'í Community

The workshop series can be publicized to the Bahá'í community through mailings to nearby Assemblies and groups, phone calls to key individuals in the area, and through local Bahá'í newsletters and Internet list serves. Flyers can be distributed at Feast, children's classes and cluster gatherings. Advance planning and repeated invitations will help to ensure good attendance. Sample Bahá'í newsletter announcements appear below, with a flyer on the following page.

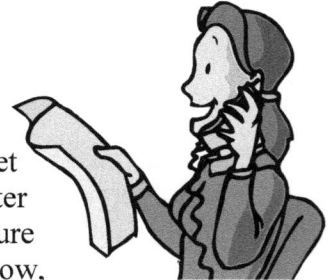

Sample announcement #1

**BAHÁ'Í PUBLIC
SPEAKING COURSE
From Panic to Proficiency**

Join us for a weekend workshop on Bahá'í Public Speaking, Sept. 19-20, from 9-5 p.m. at One World Bahá'í School.

We will share horror stories, practice basic speaking skills, learn to stand up with courage in front of a group, speak with a strong clear voice, and give a short impromptu talk.

Opportunities to speak about the Faith are multiplying. Why not get your feet wet now?

Please bring a notebook, pen and prayer book. Lunch and child care will be provided. Donations accepted. To register, call Ramin: 999-1919.

Sample announcement #2

**BAHÁ'Í PUBLIC SPEAKING
COURSE PLANNED**

"Encourage ye the school children, from their earliest years, to deliver speeches of high quality..."

('Abdu'l-Bahá: Selections, p. 134)

Beginning October 5th, Ms. Gloria Martinez will offer a nine-week Public Speaking Workshop for junior youth, ages 12-15. Participants will learn to stand up with courage in front of a group, read prayers clearly and with feeling, research the Baha'i Writings, memorize selected passages, give brief talks, answer basic questions about the Faith, develop their speaking style and much more!

Presentations can be prepared for devotional gatherings, school assignments, Feasts, firesides, Holy Days and other events.

Classes will be held at the Martinez home, every Sunday from 4-6 p.m., followed by pizza. Please bring a notebook, pen and prayer book. Come ready to learn! For more information and to sign up for the course, call 865-4321.

Bahá'í Public Speaking
Workshops for youth and campus clubs

Baha'u'llah has said that "complete victory" of the Cause
"should be achieved through speech and utterance." *

Every Tuesday for nine weeks
7:30 – 9:30 p.m.

Starts April 2nd
University Bahá'í Center
Info: 123 - 4567

Learn how to:

- Stand up with courage in front of a group
- Speak with a strong clear voice
- Present information to campus leaders
- Participate in media interviews
- Answer challenging questions
- Speak with skill and confidence about the Faith at firesides, devotionals, study circles, school events, information tables, Holy Days and public meetings

Bring a notebook, pen and prayer book.

SPONSORED BY THE LOCAL SPIRITUAL ASSEMBLY OF OUR TOWN

* Tablets of Bahá'u'lláh, p. 197

Inviting the Larger Community

Using many of the same activities, this Bahá'í-based public speaking course can be modified and offered as a service to the larger community. In workshop #1, for example, the introduction might focus on the importance of children and youth in general, rather than on the special role of Bahá'í children and youth. When listing the workshop goals, the teacher might omit the goal of presenting Bahá'í materials to community leaders. Participants can also be asked to bring their own readings and to prepare talks on a variety of subjects of particular interest to them. A sample press release is included below.

Sample press release

Bahá'ís to Offer Course in Public Speaking

I'd like to contribute my ideas for improving our community, but…
How can I stop feeling nervous when standing in front of a crowd?
How can I speak from the heart and add impact to my words?

These topics and many others will be covered during a new 9-week course being offered by the Hometown Bahá'í Community. Participants will learn how to:

- Stand up with courage in front of a group
- Speak with a strong clear voice
- Use good posture and eye contact
- Read aloud well
- Memorize passages
- Research a topic
- Write a speech
- Give a short prepared talk
- Give a short impromptu talk
- Introduce another speaker
- Speak through an interpreter
- Use a microphone

"It's definitely not boring or preachy!" says Elena Shevinsky, a high school senior who took the course last year. "I learned to conquer my fears and share my thoughts on topics that were important to me. I'm not a Bahá'í, but I really liked that the course had a spiritual foundation."

"We can all do a better job of communicating, and it's helpful to practice with others who are encouraging and positive," says Ramin Talebi, chair of the Local Spiritual Assembly of the Bahá'ís of Hometown, which is sponsoring the course as a service to the community. Mr. Talebi will help facilitate the series, which includes warm-up activities, group discussion and practice exercises.

Classes will be held from 7:00–8:30 p.m., every Monday, beginning January 9, at the Bahá'í Center, 19 Main Street. The course is free and open to anyone over 15 who is interested in increasing confidence and improving their speaking skills. To register call: 987-6543.

The author would appreciate feedback from those
who use these materials with the public.
Write to: info@UnityWorksStore.com.

FOLLOW-UP

Final Presentation

At the end of the public speaking course, a special program can be organized to provide the participants with an opportunity to demonstrate their new skills. This has been the highlight of the course for children and adults as well. The fact that they will be performing in front of a live audience serves as excellent motivation to learn the material presented during class. The Bahá'í community can be invited to the presentation, along with interested family, friends, neighbors and co-workers. Certificates of course completion can be presented if desired.

Acts of Service

In addition, the teacher, the sponsoring Assembly or cluster agencies can arrange opportunities for students to practice what they have learned long after the course. The following list suggests ideas for acts of service that will draw upon the participants' new skills.

- **Short and Sweet**

  1. Read a prayer at a Bahá'í meeting.
  2. Recite a memorized passage at a devotional gathering.
  3. Read the letter from the National Assembly at the 19-Day Feast.
  4. Share a story with a children's class.
  5. Tell a story about the Faith during a home visit.

- **Offer Your Service**

  6. Research a topic from the Bahá'í Writings.
  7. Select the readings for a devotional gathering.
  8. Help a child to memorize a Bahá'í quotation.
  9. Tutor someone in reading.
  10. Introduce the speaker at a public event.

- **Take the Challenge**

  11. Serve as a fireside speaker.
  12. Organize a youth fireside.
  13. Give a talk on the Faith at a public event.
  14. Serve as master of ceremonies for a Holy Day program.
  15. Present informational materials to public officials.
  16. Serve as a seeker response representative.
  17. Serve as a public information officer.
  18. Represent the Faith during a media interview.
  19. Work with children on a dramatic presentation.
  20. Teach the Public Speaking Course to others who are interested.

TO THE TEACHER

> **"Among the greatest of all services that can possibly be rendered by man to Almighty God is the education and training of children."**
>
> 'Abdu'l-Bahá, Selections from the Writings of 'Abdu'l-Bahá, p.133

Teacher's Guide

The teacher's guide on the following pages contains nine lesson plans for a course on Bahá'í public speaking. Participants will learn to research the Bahá'í Writings, memorize selected passages, prepare and deliver brief talks on the Faith, and develop their speaking skills. Presentations can be prepared for devotional gatherings, children's classes, study circles, firesides, Feasts, Holy Days, school assignments, public meetings and other events.

While suitable for all ages (with modifications for younger children), the course is particularly useful for youth and junior youth. The activities were developed and tested in the field, in response to the needs of teachers and children, and have been used successfully in multiple settings over many years.

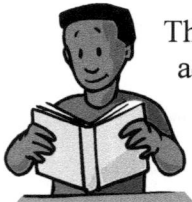

This guidebook is written in plain language, so it can be used by older youth and adults with no formal training. It includes sample publicity materials, a certificate of completion, and evaluation forms. A detailed table of contents lists the major student activities included in each lesson.

Sections on tutoring reading, memorization techniques, approaching the media, responding to controversy, and additional projects (activities for young children, ideas for dramatic presentations, and plans for a youth fireside) are included as appendices to complement the public speaking exercises.

The Lessons

The lessons are organized in a sequential, step-by-step format, each activity building on the previous one. The lessons begin with a warm-up and review questions, followed by speaking tips, practice exercises and a homework assignment.

Copy-ready student handouts are included at the end of the manual. Handouts should be photocopied (double-sided if possible) for every student and distributed during the sessions as needed. You will also need to obtain some basic educational materials such as a white board, markers and a dictionary (see list on page 5 of this guide).

Each lesson is designed to last approximately two hours, depending on the number of students and their level of ability. The suggested time for each activity is noted in parentheses after the heading. However, if students need additional time to practice a skill, or if the class is engaged in an animated discussion and wishes to continue, you can extend the time, omit part of the lesson, or save it for a future class. Be flexible.

Explanatory notes to the teacher are written in *italics*. These notes are not meant to be read as a script, but are intended only as a guide for the teacher. Key phrases and highlights from these notes can be written on the board before or during the lesson, and students can be encouraged to take their own notes as appropriate.

The first lesson in the series is written in considerable detail. It is assumed that the teacher will then understand the basic methodology and rationale, and that abbreviated explanations will be sufficient for the remaining lessons.

Additional lessons can be developed using the same pattern, based on local needs and opportunities. For example, if World Peace Day is approaching, the Assembly may ask the workshop participants to present the Mayor with a copy of "The Promise of World Peace." The students might memorize passages from that booklet, design some posters on the theme, and rehearse several times before making the formal presentation.

Similarly, the class might decide to plan a fireside, prepare a talk on community service for the local Rotary Club, host the devotional portion of Feast, put together a presentation for one of the Holy Days, organize a reception to honor their school teachers, develop a lesson for younger children at Bahá'í school, dramatize an event in Bahá'í history for a youth retreat, or select readings to recite for a interfaith worship service.

Class Discussions

During class discussions, all students should be encouraged to participate, not just the ones who speak first or loudest. An individual who is silent can be asked, "Maria, what do you think about this?" Have students raise their hands rather than shouting out the answer. A simple comment like, "I'm happy to see so many of you raising your hands quietly," will reinforce this rule.

If a student's answer is incorrect, rather than saying, "No, that's wrong," it is better to respond with, "Good try. You're on the right track," or "That's an interesting thought!" Then ask another question or give a small hint that will help that person succeed. Be patient and enthusiastic. Do not allow the participants to laugh at or tease each other.

> "It is the hope of 'Abdu'l-Bahá that those youthful souls
> ...will be tended by one who traineth them to love."
>
> Selections from the Writings of 'Abdu'l-Bahá, p.134

Student Presentations

Student presentations and practice exercises can be recorded (audio or video) if desired. These recordings can then be played back and discussed by the class. The focus should be on skills that have already been taught. While recording is not essential, it is a useful evaluation tool as it allows students to see and hear themselves.

If a podium is available, have students practice with it for some exercises and without it for others, so they feel comfortable both ways.

For presentations to groups outside the class, be sure that every student has a part, including those who seem less capable. For example, at a Holy Day celebration, even a young child can say, "Welcome to Naw-Rúz."

Critiquing the Presentations

During a critique, students should be asked to point out the positive aspects of each presentation. The teacher can take note of areas needing improvement and can work on these either individually or as a group, at that moment or at some future time. (Poor readers can be tutored separately using the guidelines in Appendix B.)

The teacher's suggestions should be phrased in a positive way, for example, "Your voice was strong and clear. Now try keeping your hands flat on the podium," rather than, "Stop twisting your shirt and biting your nails. It looks ridiculous." Encouragement is generally more motivating than criticism.

For older students, the critique can include a brief written peer evaluation if desired. Evaluation forms (page 98) can be copied as needed and distributed before each round of speeches. After each speech, the forms can be collected and given to the speaker.

Cultural Awareness

When your students are making presentations to different cultural groups, find out beforehand what is appropriate. For example, is special permission needed from either the Spiritual Assembly or from the group itself? Who should make the presentation and to whom? Is there a traditional greeting or protocol that must be observed? Are there any words or actions that would be considered disrespectful? Should gifts be exchanged first? If so, what type of gifts, and how should they be presented and received? Some advance research can prevent misunderstandings and help open doors.

Closing Thoughts

It is hoped that this manual will be a useful tool in your efforts to raise up young Bahá'í's in service to Bahá'u'lláh. May they gain the skills and confidence needed to better serve His Cause.

WORKSHOP # 1: Beginning Exercises

Materials: Handouts (including goals, story, self assessment) and 3x5 cards. Students should bring notebooks, pens and prayer books to each class. Have them write their names on the notebooks, the title of this course, the teacher's name, city and date.

---

1. WELCOME AND PRAYERS (5 min.)

2. WARMUP (5 min.)

Ask students and accept all answers.

a. How do you feel about giving a talk in front of large crowd?
b. Meeting the mayor or being interviewed on the radio or TV?
c. What experiences with public speaking have you already had?

3. INTRODUCTION (5 min.)

Paraphrase the following ideas and write key points on the board. Students can take notes.

> Bahá'í youth and children today have a special destiny before God. You are seen "as a door to entry by troops and as a fruitful source of teachers...not simply as children for whom activity must be arranged...but as a living creation of God necessary at this very moment for the purposes of God." [1]
>
> In order to build a better world with peace, unity and justice, you are called upon to share the Teachings of God for this Day. Bahá'u'lláh says that complete victory of His Cause will be achieved through speech. [2] 'Abdu'l-Bahá says that even small children should be encouraged to give speeches of high quality. [3]
>
> This workshop will prepare you to give talks and presentations as one way to teach the Faith. You can learn to do this with God's help, prayer and practice. You are not trying to become speakers just to show off your skill, but to become better servants of the Cause of God.

(1) ITC, 5 Dec 1988   (2) Tablets of Bahá'u'lláh, p.197-98   (3) Selections from 'Abdu'l-Bahá, p.134

4. SHARING THE BEAUTY OF GOD (20 min.)

Distribute handouts and have students take turns reading the story out loud. Then discuss the following questions:

a. How do you think the speaker felt about giving her talk?
b. How does she feel about the Words of Bahá'u'lláh?
c. What does she mean by comparing speaking to water?
d. What was her talk about?

Sharing the Beauty of God

by Diedre Merrill and Gayle Woolson

The room was filled with over 100 people. My friend had just completed a perfect performance on his violin. The applause of the audience sounded like thunder in my ears. Now, it was my turn.

I tried hard to concentrate on the opening sentence of my speech. I knew that once I got started, the rest of the speech would follow easily. I had practiced it so many times with my partner. I felt like a race horse, well trained and eager to start. My heart pounded in my chest. I thought of my partner reminding me to speak slowly. I must not race through my speech like a runaway stallion.

I love the words of Bahá'u'lláh. I love the way I feel when I recite them from memory. When I first looked at my speech, there were words I did not know. But my partner explained the meaning of them to me. He said the words of Bahá'u'lláh are very powerful and overflowing with wisdom. They have an effect upon the hearts of those who hear them. Now was my chance to share these words.

If I said them too fast, it would be like throwing a bucket of water at someone who was thirsty. It would quickly run off onto the floor, doing little good. If I took care to speak slowly and clearly, Bahá'u'lláh's words would have time to trickle over those in the audience with their life-giving energy.

"THE GREAT MISSION OF CHILDREN." The words exploded in my ears--the title of my speech. The eyes of my partner were filled with love as he introduced me. He was confident that I would say my speech perfectly, as I had so many times. I wanted to do my very best.

My partner told me that children like you and me, who are living in the world today, have a destiny before God. We have a very important job. We are expected to make the whole world like a single neighborhood.

'Abdu'l-Bahá said, "Love is the brightness of the beauty of God." It is up to us to share that love with everyone.

I walked to the microphone. Slowly, I began my speech. "Humanity has entered into a glorious new universal age..." Everything was going well. I saw other children in the audience. I looked at them as I continued. "We children are very fortunate to be living in this wonderful age and we have an important role to play in helping establish peace and understanding among the people of all religions, races, nations and classes."

Their eyes seemed to twinkle with excitement. Maybe they were asking, "How can we do this?" 'Abdu'l-Bahá indicated one way when He said, "Encourage ye the school children, from their earliest years, to deliver speeches of high quality." A warm feeling poured over me. I was doing just what 'Abdu'l-Bahá wanted.

I continued my speech. I was talking about the path of life that leads us towards achieving a wonderful future. I could see the wonder in people's faces as they imagined what such a future would be like. The answer was in my speech, so I hurried on.

"A magnificent view of the future is described in the Bahá'í Writings: 'the earth will be transformed; ...cooperation and union will be established; ...the human race will be like one family.'" I pictured my family, my brothers and sisters, my aunts and uncles. The picture kept growing larger and larger until it included everyone in the world.

Too quickly my speech was over. From the light shining from the faces of my partner and the others in the audience, I knew I had done well. I had shared the "brightness of the beauty of God."

(c) 1993, National Spiritual Assembly of the Bahá'ís of the United States.
From Brilliant Star Magazine. Used with permission.

5. WORKSHOP GOALS (10 min.)

Discuss the following goals with students (also listed on their handouts).

In addition to developing spiritual qualities, these workshops will help you gain practical skills and confidence. We will learn using a step-by-step approach, with lots of time for practice. Depending on your interests and the needs of the Bahá'í community, we can work on presentations for devotional gatherings, children's classes, study circles, Feasts, firesides, Holy Days, school assignments, public meetings or any other special events. My goal is that everyone in this class will have a good time and will learn to:

a. Stand up with courage in front of a group
b. Speak with a strong clear voice
c. Use good posture and eye contact
d. Read aloud well
e. Memorize Bahá'í passages
f. Answer questions about the Faith
g. Research a topic from the Writings
h. Write a speech
i. Give a short prepared talk
j. Give a short impromptu talk *(unrehearsed)*
k. Introduce another speaker
l. Present Bahá'í materials to local officials*
m. Speak through an interpreter *(language translator)*
n. Use a microphone
o. Be interviewed by the media

6. SELF ASSESSMENT (15 min.)

Tell the class that the purpose of evaluation is to help each student become a more effective communicator. Explain that we will evaluate each other at the end of each speech. We will also evaluate ourselves at the beginning, middle and end of the course. Then distribute the self-assessment (pages 68-69) and have students use pencils to complete the forms for day one. When finished, collect the forms.

7. ASSIGNMENT (5 min.)

☐ Choose a partner to practice with outside of class: _____

Students can practice in person or by phone. They might choose a parent or another adult from the community, or a friend from this class. Have them write the names of one or two possible partners on their handouts now.

☐ Schedule a time to practice: _____

For example, they might decide to call each other every Sunday at 4 p.m.

8. BEGINNING EXERCISES (35 min.)

Are you ready to begin? We'll practice these exercises one at a time until you feel comfortable. Each one gets a little harder. Everyone will perform the first skill at the front of the room. We'll repeat it until you can all do it well. Then you can check it off on your handout and we'll go on to the next skill. I'll demonstrate each item first. If you have already mastered a skill, others will be able to learn from watching you practice. Remember, no laughing or teasing. We're all here to learn, and our purpose is to serve God. Let's encourage each other. Okay? Now, who wants to go first?

> **Note:** Each item incorporates the previous ones. For example, the first skill is walking to the front of the room and back. For the second skill, students should walk to the front of the room, stand facing the audience for three seconds, then walk back. The third skill involves walking up and back, standing for three seconds, plus a self introduction.

☐ **Walk to the front and back in a relaxed, dignified manner**

Pay attention to pace, posture, facial expression and hands.
Arms should swing loosely at your sides.

☐ **Stand facing the audience with good posture
and eye contact for three seconds**

This 'three-second rule' applies both before and after any public talk.
It gives you a chance to take a deep breath, say a silent prayer, collect your thoughts, and make eye contact with the audience before you begin.
It also puts a frame of silence around your talk, and keeps you from speaking on the way to and from the podium, when you are not likely to be heard.

☐ **Introduce yourself (name, age, town)**

Example: "My name is Zia. I'm eleven years old and I live in Yakima, Washington." Avoid biting your lips, wringing your hands, twisting your clothes, etc. Remember the three-second rule both before and after your introduction. During your talk, look directly at various members of the audience for a few moments each, so no one will feel left out. (In certain cultures, this may not be appropriate, so check first.)

☐ **Introduce another speaker**

Work in pairs to select a topic that you might like to give a speech about some day. Take turns introducing each other. Remember good posture, eye contact, and the three-second rule. Older students might first welcome the audience. For example: "Welcome to the Bahá'í youth conference. Our first speaker is Jonathan Kalim. Jonathan is fifteen years old and his topic is 'Youth Can Move the World.' Please join me in welcoming him."

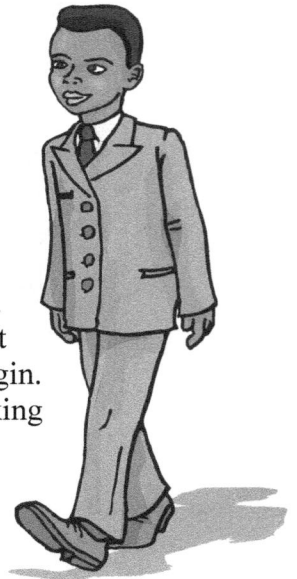

9. TONE OF VOICE (10 min.)

You can add drama and realism to your speech by varying the tone of your voice. For example, say all the sentences below, first in a monotone, then with appropriate emotion and emphasis.

Have class repeat after you in unison:

> - **I'm really angry.**   - **I'm really sad.**   - **I'm really embarrassed.**   - **I'm really happy.**

Now repeat the last sentence, but give it a different meaning each time. *(Examples: truly happy, sarcastic, questioning, insistent, I am but they're not ...)* This shows that tone of voice carries the real meaning and is even more important than your words.

10. HOMEWORK: Observe newscast

Ask students to watch a television news show for about ten minutes.

a. Listen to each announcer's tone of voice.

b. Watch their lip and mouth movements.

c. Can you understand each word?

d. Pay attention to pauses.

e. Where are their eyes looking?

f. Observe their posture and facial expressions.

g. Describe their hair and clothing.

h. Take notes and be ready to share what you have learned.

11. ONE-MINUTE FEEDBACK

Give each student a 3x5 card. They should not put their names on the cards. Ask them to write one thing they learned today, one thing they liked most about the lesson, and one suggestion for improvement. Collect the cards. Share a few highlights with the class next time, and use this information to improve your class in the future. (Note: This activity is listed at the end of each lesson as a reminder, but it is not necessary to do every time.)

I learned:

I liked:

I suggest:

Remind them to choose a partner and arrange a time to practice.

Self Assessment Sample

Date: _____ (first day of course)	→ Use pencil
Date: _____ (halfway through course)	→ Use blue pen
Date: _____ (last day of course)	→ Use red pen

Name: _____   Teacher: _____

(1) How comfortable do you feel?
(Circle one number for each item)

		Very Un-comfortable		In the Middle		Very Comfortable
a.	Standing in front of a group	①	2	3	4	5
b.	Speaking with a strong clear voice	1	②	3	4	5
c.	Using good posture and eye contact	①	2	3	4	5
d.	Reading aloud	1	2	③	4	5
e.	Memorizing Bahá'í passages	1	2	③	4	5
f.	Answering questions about the Faith	1	②	3	4	5
g.	Researching a topic from the Writings	1	②	3	4	5
h.	Writing a speech	①	2	3	4	5
i.	Giving a short prepared talk	①	2	3	4	5
j.	Giving a short impromptu talk	①	2	3	4	5
k.	Introducing another speaker	1	②	3	4	5
l.	Presenting items to community leaders	①	2	3	4	5
m.	Speaking through an interpreter	①	2	3	4	5
n.	Using a microphone	①	2	3	4	5
o.	Being interviewed by the media	①	2	3	4	5

(2) Connect the circles.

(3) Tell me about yourself as a public speaker. (Use back of page)

Self Assessment Sample, page 2

First day of course:

Halfway through course:

Last day of course:

WORKSHOP # 2: Speaking Style

Materials: Handouts, feedback from previous lesson, 3x5 cards.

---

1. **WELCOME AND PRAYERS** (2 min.)

2. **SHARE FEEDBACK** (3 min.)

   Share excerpts or summarize responses from 3x5 cards.

3. **REVIEW PREVIOUS LESSON** (10 min.)

   a. How can Bahá'í youth and children teach the Faith?
   b. What are some of the goals of these workshops?
   c. What is the proper attitude for a Bahá'í speaker?
   d. What presentation skills did we learn last time? →

   > walk, posture, eye contact, hands, three-second rule, introductions, tone of voice

   e. Why is the three-second "frame" important?

4. **HOMEWORK CHECK** (10 min.)

   a. Partner's name and practice schedule? *(Ask each student and record info.)*
   b. Observations from the TV newscast?

5. **EXERCISES** (45 min.) *(Distribute handouts. Have students stand at their seats.)*

   ☐ Relaxation techniques *(Before going up: shake, stretch, deep breaths, pray.)*
   ☐ State name with three-second frame *(Have students do this, one at a time, first with poor posture; then a second time with shoulders back and chin up.)*

   Repeat each sentence twice as indicated:

   ☐ Sentence A: weak voice / strong voice
   ☐ Sentence B: with a big ego in your voice / with an attitude of service
   ☐ Sentence C: mumbled words / clearly pronounced words
   ☐ Sentence D: eyes down / good eye contact
   ☐ Sentence E: monotone / melodious voice
   ☐ Sentence F: too fast / too slow / just right

   ### Sentences for Practice Exercises

   A. Good evening friends. Welcome to our Holy Day celebration.
   B. Our community is pleased to present the Bahá'í Youth Workshop.
   C. The Youth Workshop is a group of young Bahá'ís who are sharing a message of unity through their music and dance.
   D. Unity is one of the most important teachings of the Baha'i Faith.
   E. After the performance, we invite you to stay for refreshments and we will be glad to answer any questions you might have.
   F. And now, the Bahá'í Youth Workshop.

6. CHARACTERISTICS OF A GOOD PUBLIC SPEAKER (20 min.)

Draw a grid on the board. Ask students to suggest some of the elements we can use to evaluate a public speaker, e.g., posture, voice, eye contact, knowledge of subject matter, organization, attitude, etc. Write in items across the top of the grid as suggested by students. Give them hints if they are slow in coming up with ideas.

	Posture	Voice	Eye Contact	Attitude	Etc. →

Then in the left column, add three levels of speaking ability (Beginning, Intermediate, Advanced). Ask: What does a beginning speaker look and sound like? Fill in the grid with the characteristics suggested by students (e.g. poor posture, soft voice, mumbles, looks down, very nervous, unprepared, speaks too fast, etc.) Do the same for the Intermediate and Advanced levels. Students may wish to take notes.

	Posture	Voice	Eye Contact	Attitude	Etc. →
BEGINNING SPEAKER	poor bent over	too soft mumbles speaks fast	looks down	nervous	
INTERMEDIATE SPEAKER					
ADVANCED SPEAKER					

After completing the grid, ask students what level they feel they are at now. What would it take to move up a level? Encourage discussion. This exercise will help students develop an understanding of where they are, where they are headed, and what they need to do to get there.

7. DISCUSSION (5 min.)

Ask the class:

- How does the speaker's presentation style (voice, posture, eye contact, etc.) affect the audience?

- How does it affect the speaker?

8. MEMORIZATION (20 min.)

Students should memorize all or part of the quote below. Younger students might only work on the first phrase. (See Appendix C for memorization techniques.) Use the backwards buildup technique for this lesson. Have students repeat after you, then practice in pairs. Allow about ten minutes for practice, and another ten for reciting in front of the class.

Ask for volunteers: "Who thinks they can recite the entire passage with no mistakes?" If the more capable students go first, they will serve as role models for the others, who will hear the passage several times before it is their turn. If they make mistakes, let them try again after hearing the passage a few more times. Remember good posture, voice control and the three-second frame.

✴

"Now is the time to speak forth
and to deliver speeches,
the time to teach and to give testimony.
Loosen thy tongue...
The Holy Spirit speaketh
through the innermost essence
of the human tongue..."

'Abdu'l-Bahá, Women, p.398

9. HOMEWORK: Memorize a quote

Have students select one of the eight quotations from the back of the handout. They should look up the meaning of any words they don't know, then memorize the quote with their partner's help, and be prepared to recite it next time.

10. ONE-MINUTE FEEDBACK *(Same as in Workshop #1, using 3x5 cards.)*

QUOTATIONS ON SPEECH

Select one or more of the following quotations to memorize. Look up the meaning of any words you don't know. Practice with your partner and be ready to recite next time. Use good posture, eye contact, voice control and a three-second frame.

(1) "This is the day in which to speak…Within every word a new spirit is hidden." *(Bahá'u'lláh: quoted in Advent of Divine Justice, p. 69)*

(2) "We have ordained that complete victory should be achieved through speech and utterance…" *(Bahá'u'lláh: Tablets of Bahá'u'lláh, p. 197-198)*

(3) "Encourage ye the school children, from their earliest years, to deliver speeches of high quality…" *('Abdu'l-Bahá: Selections, p. 134)*

(4) "It is the hope of 'Abdu'l-Bahá that those youthful souls…even as a nightingale endowed with speech, will cry out the secrets of the Heavenly Realm." *('Abdu'l-Bahá: Selections, p. 134)*

(5) "Grant, O my God, that I may not be reckoned among those whose ears are deaf, whose eyes are blind, whose tongues are speechless and whose hearts have failed to comprehend." *(Selections from the Báb, p. 216)*

(6) "Whoso openeth his lips in this day, and maketh mention of the name of his Lord, the hosts of Divine inspiration shall descend upon him from the heaven of My name, the All-Knowing, the All-Wise. On him shall also descend the Concourse on high, each bearing aloft a chalice of pure light." *(Bahá'u'lláh: quoted in Advent of Divine Justice, p. 71)*

(7) "From the texts of the wondrous, heavenly Scriptures they should memorize phrases and passages…so that in the course of their speech they may recite divine verses whenever the occasion demandeth it, inasmuch as these holy verses are the most potent elixir, the greatest and mightiest talisman. So potent is their influence that the hearer will have no cause for vacillation." *(Bahá'u'lláh: Tablets of Bahá'u'lláh, p. 200)*

(8) "It is my earnest hope that you…may be so enkindled by the flame set ablaze by the hand of God as to illumine the whole world through the quickening energy of the love of God, and that through the eloquence of your speech, the fluency of your tongue, and the confirmations of the Holy Spirit you will be empowered to expound divine wisdom in such manner that men of eloquence, and the scholars and sages of the world, will be lost in bewilderment." *(Shoghi Effendi: Bahiyyih Khanum, p. 100)*

WORKSHOP # 3: Basic Presentations

Materials: Handouts, feedback, 3x5 cards, small prizes for each student (see #3 below), books to use as props (#6), and pamphlets on race unity (#7).

---

1. WELCOME AND PRAYERS (2 min.)

2. SHARE FEEDBACK AND REVIEW PREVIOUS LESSON (8 min.)

a. List several ways to relax before giving a talk. *(Shake, stretch, breathe, pray...)*

b. Name some elements of speech and explain why each is important. *(Volume, speed, pronunciation, tone of voice, attitude...)*

3. HOMEWORK CHECK: Memorized quote (10 min.)

Students should recite quotes they have memorized. Remember good posture, eye contact, voice control and three-second frame. Consider offering each a small reward (candy, Bahá'í postcard or photo) and some applause for their efforts.

4. ONE-MINUTE TALK (50 min.)

☐ Give a one-minute talk on "What is the Bahá'í Faith?"

Ask the students: What is the Bahá'í Faith? Go around the room and have each person give a short one-sentence answer. Each should add something new. Take notes on the board. Go around again if there are more ideas.

Consult on which of these points might be included in a brief introductory talk. Then have students work in pairs to prepare a one-minute answer to the question. They can paraphrase it or read from their notes. Allow fifteen minutes for writing and practice. They should time their answers and revise to fit the limit. Both members of each pair should give the talk.

Facilitate a positive critique after each presentation, e.g. "What were some of the positive things you noticed about LaTasha's speech?" If, as the teacher, you wish to offer a suggestion for improvement, either privately or in front of the group, sandwich it between two positive comments.

5. SPEAKING FROM THE HEART (5 min.)

Ask students which has greater impact and why.
Demonstrate each one.

(A)

The speaker stands behind a podium, reading from notes and glancing only occasionally at the audience.

(B)

The speaker makes eye contact, speaks from the heart, and glances only occasionally at his or her notes.

Reading from notes or reciting a memorized speech can sound stiff and distant. Speaking from the heart sounds more natural and creates a closer connection with the audience. To minimize reliance on notes, we will be using keywords and simple pictures to remind us of what to say, rather than writing out our speeches word for word.

6. LIBRARY BOOK PRESENTATION (45 min.)

☐ Draw a pictoscript

Students will practice a book presentation using the sample script below. First, distribute 3x5 cards and have students make a simple drawing to remind them of each point in the script. They can refer to this "pictoscript" when presenting the book, but should use their own words, without memorization or notes.

Sample Script

- On behalf of the Bahá'í community, we would like to present this Spanish children's book to the library. ⟶

- The book (El Regalo) is about animals who are always fighting because they follow different religious teachings. ⟶

- Then a dove brings them a new book and they learn to live together in peace. ⟶

Sample Pictoscript

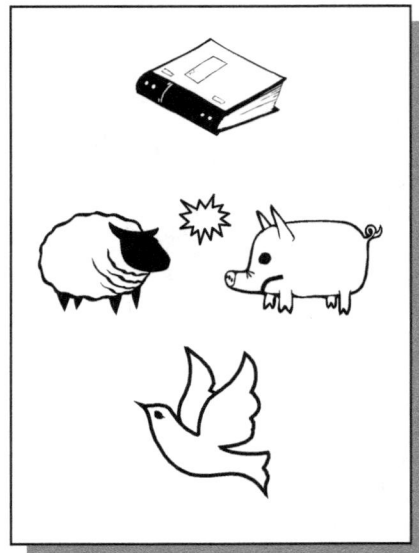

☐ Library book presentation
☐ Mini-interview with the librarian

Students should practice in pairs, taking turns acting as the librarian. They should use their pictoscripts and any book as a prop. After practicing for about ten minutes, have them switch partners. Then ask each new pair to come to the front, and take turns presenting the book and answering the librarian's question. The answer should be impromptu (unrehearsed), but they can draw on ideas from the one-minute answer they prepared earlier.

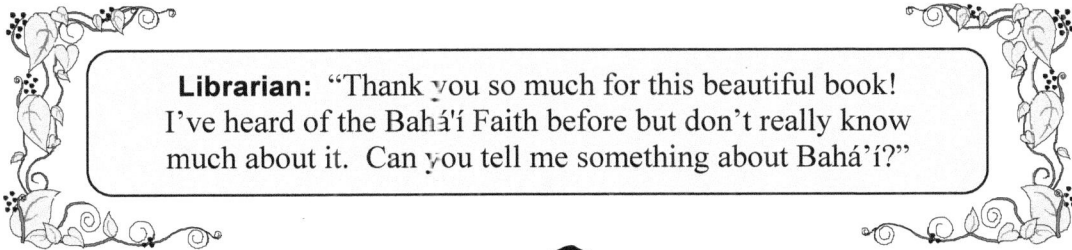

Librarian: "Thank you so much for this beautiful book! I've heard of the Bahá'í Faith before but don't really know much about it. Can you tell me something about Bahá'í?"

7. HOMEWORK: One-minute talk on race unity

Have students prepare a one-minute talk on the Bahá'í principle of race unity, including a short memorized quote from the Writings. The speech itself should not be memorized, but students can use a pictoscript or keywords if desired. For example, in the library presentations, the keywords "book," "fighting animals" and "dove" might be listed on a 3x5 card. Students can rehearse with a partner, in front of a mirror, or using an audio recorder. Distribute pamphlets on race unity for students to take home for ideas. They should take notes or underline key points as they read.

8. ONE-MINUTE FEEDBACK (Use 3x5 cards)

WORKSHOP # 4: Answering Questions

Materials: Handouts, feedback, question sets (see #5, #6), 3x5 cards.

1. WELCOME AND PRAYERS (2 min.)

2. SHARE FEEDBACK AND REVIEW (8 min.)

a. Describe the "backwards buildup" technique for memorizing.
b. What is a "pictoscript"?

3. GREETINGS AND INTRODUCTIONS (10 min.)

Most talks should begin with some type of courtesy greeting, rather than starting cold. This serves to acknowledge the audience and provides a smoother opening. Students might recall one famous greeting from history: "Friends, Romans, countrymen, lend me your ears..." (Marc Antony speaking at Caesar's funeral in Shakespeare's Julius Caesar.) Other examples include: My fellow Americans...; Parents, teachers, classmates...; Participants in our Book 4 study circle; Members of the Rotary Club...

☐ Greet the audience
☐ Introduce the speaker

Ask students to work in pairs. They should practice greeting the audience and introducing each other for the race unity speech.

The introduction should include the speaker's name, topic and anything interesting about the speaker of relevance to the talk.

> Example: "Members of the public speaking class: I would like to introduce Jamal Johnson who will speak to you on the important topic of race unity. Jamal grew up in a multi-racial family and has a lot of interesting experiences to share. Please join me in welcoming him."

Introducers should stand at the front of the room, using the same strong voice, good posture and eye contact as for any speech. After the introduction, they can shake the speaker's hand, step away from the front and lead the applause. After the speech, the introducer can return to the front, thank the speaker, shake hands and clap once more. It is best not to leave the front of the room empty. Either the speaker or the introducer should be there. Have students practice these introductions at their seats in preparation for the next activity.

4. HOMEWORK CHECK (35 min.)

☐ One-minute talk on race unity

Using the same pairs from the exercise above, have each student greet the audience and introduce his or her partner, who will share the one-minute prepared speech on race unity. Appoint a time-keeper to record the minutes and seconds of each speech (see Appendix D). Conduct a positive critique after each talk, and when all the talks are completed, call for the timekeeper's report.

5. ANSWERING QUESTIONS: Prepared Response (30 min.)

☐ Prepared response (list A or B)

There are three lists of questions for Workshop #4. Keep them separate. Photocopy each list once onto a different colored card stock. Laminate if desired, and cut on the dotted lines. Put each set of questions into a separate box or hat, and label the boxes A, B and C.

The questions on List A ask about basic Bahá'í teachings. The questions on List B are more challenging. Decide which list is more appropriate for your students, or develop your own set of questions. If desired, you could have both sets of questions available and give students the option of choosing from the easier or the more difficult box.

> Note: Additional questions and answers can be found in Dale Eng's wonderful reference book, *Responding: 101 Questions Often Asked of Bahá'ís,* available from the Bahá'í Distribution Service (www.BahaiBookStore.com) or from Exir Publishing (www.exirpublishing.com).

> If the course is being offered as a service to the public, rather than answering a set of prepared questions on the Bahá'í Faith, you might have students each make up a question or two to add to the box. They should print legibly on 3x5 cards, and should not include their names.

Have students work in pairs. Each pair should pull one question from the box. Give them about fifteen minutes to research the question and prepare a short (1-2 min.) answer. Provide pamphlets and reference works. Have students take brief notes on 3x5 cards, listing one idea per card (see example below). They should not write out or memorize the talk. Have them number the cards so they stay in order. For example, a brief talk on progressive revelation might use the following cards:

-1- Progressive Revelation	-2- Names of Prophets	-3- Like sun in mirror	-4- Like teachers in school

Appoint a new timekeeper. When presenting, go in order starting with question #1. Have each pair greet the audience, read the question, then answer it. They should alternate—each member of the pair sharing a part of the answer. Remember good posture, voice control, eye contact, etc. End with positive critiques and timekeeper's report.

6. ANSWERING QUESTIONS: Impromptu Response (30 min.)

☐ Impromptu response (list C)

Appoint new timekeeper. Using the same pairs, have one partner greet the audience, then select a list-C question from the box, read it and introduce the other partner, who will give a short (1-2 min.) spontaneous answer (no research or preparation).

For example:

Mrs. Martinez and members of the speech class:

The first question is... **'How does your family feel about you becoming a Bahá'í?'**

My partner, Mr. Benedetto, will now share his thoughts on this interesting topic.

Before responding, students should pause briefly to organize their thoughts. After the talk, others may add comments, if desired. Continue, with each student drawing a question for his or her partner, one at a time in any order. This exercise gives students an opportunity to "think on their feet," while at the same time highlighting the benefits of advance preparation. If time allows, students may wish to replace questions in the box and repeat the exercise. End with positive critiques and a timekeeper's report.

7. HOMEWORK: Prepare a two-minute talk for a Bahá'í fireside

Students should each choose a topic for a two-minute fireside talk. The topic should be one that has meaning—something they feel strongly about and can talk about with sincerity, enthusiasm and conviction. Students should research the topic and write key words or draw a pictoscript on 3x5 cards, using one or more ideas per card. Students should memorize at least one quote on the topic, without memorizing the speech itself. They should practice at home and be prepared to give the speech next time.

8. ONE-MINUTE FEEDBACK

Common questions about the Bahá'í Faith for workshop #4

(Keep lists separate. Copy onto card stock, laminate if desired, and cut on dotted lines.)

1. What is the Bahá'í Faith?

6. Who is the leader of the Bahá'í Faith now?

2. Who is Bahá'u'lláh?

7. What do Bahá'ís believe about life after death?

3. How many Bahá'ís are there in the world? The country? Our town?

8. What do Bahá'ís believe about the future of the world?

4. What are the main teachings of the Bahá'í Faith?

9. What do Bahá'ís believe about Jesus?

5. How did the Bahá'í Faith begin?

10. If all religions come from the same God, why are they all so different?

Challenging questions about the Bahá'í Faith for workshop #4
(Keep lists separate. Copy onto card stock, laminate if desired, and cut on dotted lines.)

1. How do you know God exists?

2. Why do we need another religion when we already have so many?

3. What's new or different about the Bahá'í Faith?

4. It sounds too idealistic. What makes you think you can change the world?

5. I like the Bahá'í principles, but why do I have to join an organized religion?

6. What are Bahá'ís actually doing to make the world a better place?

7. Do Bahá'ís believe in creation or evolution?

8. If there is a God, how can He let so many bad things happen?

9. Everyone thinks their religion is right. What makes you so sure the Bahá'í Faith is true?

10. Are you saved?

Personal questions about the Bahá'í Faith for workshop #4
(Keep lists separate. Copy onto card stock, laminate if desired, and cut on dotted lines.)

1. How did you become a Bahá'í?

2. Name one Bahá'í teaching you especially like and why.

3. Tell about the first person in your family to become a Bahá'í.

4. How would the world be different if all people became Bahá'ís?

5. How would your life be different if you had never heard of the Faith?

6. The main teaching of Bahá'u'lláh is world unity. What do you think the main teaching of the next Manifestation will be?

7. What would happen if the mayor of your town became a Bahá'í?

8. How would popular music, movies and computer games be different if the producers were Bahá'ís?

9. What is your favorite Bahá'í song and why?

10. If you could choose any occasion or place in the world to give a talk on the Bahá'í Faith, where would it be?

WORKSHOP # 5: Organizing a Speech

Materials: Handouts, feedback, self-assessment from workshop #1, 3x5 cards.

---

1. WELCOME AND PRAYERS (2 min.)

2. FEEDBACK AND REVIEW (8 min.)

a. What are some differences between a prepared talk and an impromptu talk?

b. What are some ways to prepare for a talk? ➝

c. Give examples of an audience greeting at the start of a speech, and explain why this is helpful.

d. What information should be included when introducing a speaker?

> Pray, study topic, notes on 3x5 cards, keywords or pictoscript, memorize relevant quotes, rehearse with partner or mirror, record your talk and play it back several times, relaxation techniques.

3. HOMEWORK CHECK: Two-minute fireside talk (45 min.)

Appoint timekeeper and "fill word" counter (see Appendix D). Assign different students to introduce each speaker. Remind speakers to begin with a greeting to the audience. Share and critique the fireside talks. When all speeches are finished, share timekeeper and "fill word" counter reports.

4. PURPOSE OF A SPEECH: (5 min.)

Have students read aloud from handout.

?

Every speech should be planned with the end result in mind. Ask yourself: Why am I giving this speech? What is the topic and why is it important to me?

You must also think about your topic from the audience's point of view. Why is the topic important to them? How does it affect their family, their neighborhood or community? How can you present your ideas so the audience will clearly understand your point of view?

What do you want the audience to do as a result of hearing your speech? Do you want them to attend a fireside? Host a Feast? Contribute to the Fund? Plan a devotional meeting? Organize a service project?

Are you trying to inform? Persuade? Inspire? Entertain? Be specific. Recommend solutions. Issue a call to action. Don't just let your speech begin and end in words.

5. MATCHING EXERCISE (10 min.)

Each excerpt below comes from a different speech. On their handouts, have students match each excerpt with the presumed purpose of the presentation. Share. Some excerpts may fit more than one category. In case of disagreement, ask students to justify their choices.

Excerpt		Purpose of Presentation
(1) We hope you enjoyed our talent show. Thank you for coming.	_2_	INFORM
(2) On behalf of the Bahá'í community, we would like to present you with this booklet on race unity.	_4_	PERSUADE
(3) This story shows how, even with no money, just a few sincere Bahá'ís can achieve great victories for the Faith.	_5_	CALL TO ACTION
(4) We already know that the most effective way to teach is through personal firesides. So let's give it a try!	_3_	INSPIRE
(5) We need everyone to sign up for the service project this weekend.	_1_	ENTERTAIN

6. ORGANIZING A SPEECH (15 min.)

This section is intended for older students who have had experience writing essays in school. Younger students may need assistance. Highlight key points on the board as students read aloud.

Once you have selected a topic and decided on the purpose of your speech, you will need to organize your ideas. Good organization is one key to an effective speech. When planning a car trip, it is important to bring a road map and to mark your destination with points of interest along the route.

Every speech should have a road map as well. The audience needs to know where they are going and how they will get there, or they may become lost and confused. There are many ways to organize a speech. One way is to divide the speech into three parts: a beginning, middle and end.

- **The beginning section introduces the topic.** It tells the audience what the speech will be about and the main points you plan to cover. Using the car trip analogy, this is like saying: We are driving to the Bahá'í House of Worship and we will pass Kansas City, St. Louis and Chicago along the way.

- **The middle section is the main body of the speech.** It should include two or three main points. For each point, you should provide facts, examples, stories or quotes to support your views. The body of the speech should follow some kind of order (logical, chronological, cause and effect, comparison and contrast, etc.) This is like a road map for the audience.

- **The final section should summarize what the speech was about.** It can include your recommendations and a call to action. This is like the destination of the car trip.

To summarize: First tell them what you will say, say it, then tell them what you said. Two examples are included below. *(Have students read aloud.)*

Example A

Beginning: Welcome to our final class on becoming a Bahá'í. This morning we will review the basic Bahá'í teachings, the three Central Figures of the Faith, some laws and the Administrative Order. These are the essential elements of Bahá'í belief.

Middle: Let's start with the basic teachings. The first teaching is… (etc.)

End: That completes the class on becoming a Bahá'í. We reviewed the basic Bahá'í teachings, the three Central Figures of the Faith, some laws and the Administrative Order. We are delighted that you have all accepted these essential elements of Bahá'í belief, and have decided to join the Bahá'í Faith. Welcome!

Ask: What is the purpose of this speech? What is the topic? What are the main points? Why do you think the audience would be interested? What is the call to action?

Example B

Beginning: This evening, I will share the Bahá'í teaching on progressive revelation. We will learn that God never leaves mankind alone. In every age, He sends us Prophets to teach us how to live together and to worship Him.

Middle: A new Prophet comes every 500-1,000 years. Each one gives us a little more knowledge, just like teachers in a school. The first Prophet I will speak about is Abraham. Abraham was like the teacher for first grade. He taught that …(etc.)

End: That's how God talks to humanity. He never leaves us alone. He sends His Prophets to teach us how to live together and to worship Him. Just like teachers in a school, each one brings us something new. Bahá'ís call this progressive revelation. Are there any questions?

Ask: What is the purpose of this speech? What is the topic? What are the main points? Why do you think the audience would be interested? What is the call to action?

7. EXERCISES (20 min.)

Have students complete these exercises on their handouts.
They may work in pairs if desired. Share after each one.

A. Put sentences in logical order.

(Put a #1 by the sentence that should go first, etc.)

[2]   You will need flour, sugar, butter, oatmeal and raisins.
[4]   After mixing ingredients, spoon dough onto cookie sheet.
[3]   Before making the dough, pre-heat oven to 350 degrees.
[5]   Bake for 12 minutes; let cool and enjoy.
[1]   To bake Ayyám-i-Há cookies, first assemble the ingredients.

B. Put sentences in chronological order.

[5]   Bahá'u'lláh is God's most recent Messenger, declaring his mission in 1863.
[3]   The Jewish Holy Book is called the Torah.
[1]   The Hindu faith began in India with Krishna about 2,000 years before Christ.
[4]   Christianity began with the birth of Jesus about the year 1 A.D.
[2]   Next came Moses and the Jewish faith at around 1,300 BC in Egypt

C. Add beginning and ending sections to the middle paragraph below.

Middle: The devotional part of the Feast consists of prayers and readings from the Holy Writings. These can be chanted or set to music if desired. The business portion of the Feast provides time for the Bahá'í community to consult on matters of interest, to hear reports and to offer recommendations to the Local Spiritual Assembly. The social portion of Feast is the time when the believers can enjoy refreshments and fellowship, associating with each other in a spirit of love and unity.

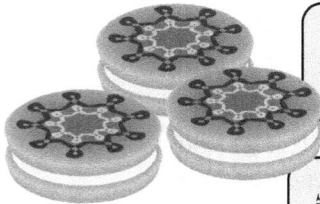

Sample beginning: The 19-Day Feast has three parts: the devotional portion, the business portion and the social portion.

Sample ending: The Feast, with its devotional, business and social portions, provides a great opportunity for the Bahá'í community to come together every 19 days. I hope to see you at the next Feast!

Ask: What is the purpose of this speech? What is the topic? What are the main points?
Why do you think the audience would be interested? What is the call to action?

8. HOMEWORK: Three-minute fireside talk

Re-write your fireside speech (or choose a new topic). First decide on the purpose of your speech and your own point of view. Then determine the audience's interest. Organize the speech with a beginning, middle and ending. Include two or three main points with the facts, examples, stories or quotes to support your views. Include an appeal to action at the end. Use the sample outline below as a guide. Make notes using keywords or pictures on 3x5 cards. Time your speech. It should be approximately three minutes long. Practice in front of a mirror and with your partner. Be ready for the next class. Good luck!

Sample outline for a speech

A. Beginning
  1. Attract audience attention
  2. Introduce topic

B. Middle
  1. First point
      a. Fact or example
      b. Fact or example
  2. Second point
      a. Fact or example
      b. Fact or example
  3. Third point
      a. Fact or example
      b. Fact or example

C. Ending
  1. Summary and conclusion
  2. Call to action

9. SELF ASSESSMENT (10 min.)

Re-distribute the assessment forms. Have students complete the form for "halfway through" using a blue pen. Collect again.

10. ONE-MINUTE FEEDBACK

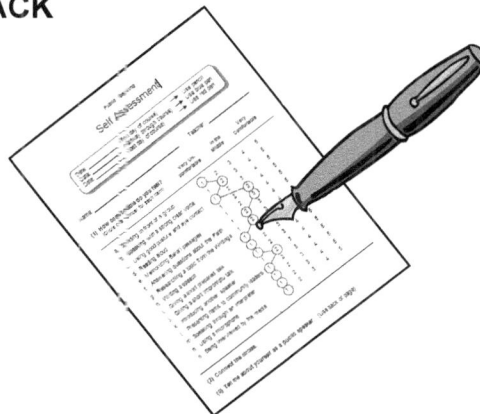

WORKSHOP # 6: Touching the Hearts

Materials: Handouts, feedback, 3x5 cards.

---

1. WELCOME AND PRAYERS (2 min.)

2. FEEDBACK AND REVIEW (8 min.)

a. What are some of the purposes of a speech?
    (inform, persuade, inspire, entertain, call to action)

b. How is organizing a speech like planning a road trip?

c. Explain one way to organize a speech. *(beginning, middle, end)*

d. What does each section contain? *(see workshop #5, item #6)*

3. HOMEWORK CHECK: Three-minute fireside talk (45 min.)

Appoint timekeeper and fill counter. Assign different students to introduce each speaker. Remind speakers to begin with a greeting to the audience. Share and critique three-minute fireside talks based on sample outline from workshop #5. Students can also listen for tone of voice, clarity of pronunciation and other elements of a good speech. If desired, these talks can be recorded and replayed individually or at a separate session. When all speeches are finished, share reports from the timekeeper and fill counter.

4. OPENINGS AND CLOSINGS (5 min.)

A good opening line should grab the audience's attention and identify the topic of the speech. The opening, ***"Today I'm going to talk about prejudice,"*** identifies the topic, but it isn't too exciting. A better opening might be, ***"What if all the children in the world were born without prejudice?"*** A catchy opening might consist of a question, a surprising statistic, a challenging statement, a memorable quote, a joke, a story, a colorful picture or graph.

A good closing should tie everything together and summarize the main points of the speech. It might relate back to the opening question and provide the answer. For example: ***"What if all the children in the world were born without prejudice? They are!"*** The closing might include a poem, a quotation or an appeal for action. One famous speech about freedom (by Patrick Henry in 1775) ended with the rousing exclamation, ***"Give me liberty or give me death!"***

It is a good idea to memorize the opening and closing lines. This will increase your confidence and ensure a strong start and finish to your speech.

5. EXERCISE (20 min.)

☐ Write memorable opening and closing lines for each topic below. Be creative!

Give students time to work individually for a few minutes (use handout). Then have them work together in small groups. When finished, ask them to share all the opening lines, then all the closing lines, one topic at a time. Write their suggestions on the board.

a. Martyrdom of the Báb ⟶

b. Bahá'í Elections

c. The Bahá'í Fund

d. Equality of Women and Men

> **Example**
>
> Opening: "Bullets from 750 rifles couldn't stop Him!"
>
> Closing: "From merchant, to Messenger of God, to martyr— the short life of the Báb had ended."

6. DIFFUSING THE DIVINE FRAGRANCES (25 min.)

To be successful in "diffusing the Divine fragrances" we need more than public speaking skills. We must also develop spiritual qualities, reliance on God and a radiant heart. The audience will hear the spirit of a talk more than the words. Before we speak, we must first teach our own selves.

Have the class read aloud each quote on the student handout (see below).

Students should look up any unfamiliar terms in the dictionary. Ask them to summarize the meaning of each passage in their own words. Discuss how these passages might apply to the students in this workshop.

(A) "Let them, at the very outset, teach their own selves, that their speech may attract the hearts of their hearers." *(Bahá'u'lláh, quoted in Advent of Divine Justice, p. 60)*

(B) "'Abdu'l-Bahá has stressed that when Bahá'ís deliver their speeches in gatherings, they are to do so in an attitude of utmost humility and self-abnegation." *(Kitáb-i-Aqdas: Notes, p. 236)*

(C) "The heavenly glad tidings must be delivered with the utmost dignity and magnanimity." *('Abdu'l-Bahá: Selections, p. 160)*

(D) "With hearts overflowing with the love of God, with souls gladdened by the heavenly glad-tidings, and with extreme humility and lowliness, let them speak out with eloquent speech, and praise and glorify the Great Lord..." *('Abdu'l-Bahá: Women, p. 396-397)*

(E) "The teacher, when teaching, must be himself fully enkindled, so that his utterance, like unto a flame of fire, may exert influence and consume the veil of self and passion. ...so that he may teach with the melody of the Concourse on high - otherwise his teaching will have no effect." *('Abdu'l-Bahá: Selections, p. 270)*

(F) "O thou maid-servant of God! Whenever thou art intending to deliver a speech, turn thy face toward the Kingdom of ABHA and, with a heart detached, begin to talk. The breaths of the Holy Spirit will assist thee." *(Tablets of 'Abdu'l-Bahá, vol. 2, 1930 printing, p. 246)*

7. MEMORIZATION (10 min.)

Select one of the above quotes for the class to memorize. Teach them the "eraser" technique described in Appendix C. Give them time to practice. When everyone appears ready, ask for volunteers. (See workshop 2, #8.)

Let them, at the very outset, teach their own selves

8. HOMEWORK: Virtue story

Another way to organize a speech is through the use of stories. Stories can be based on the experiences of people or animals. The characters can be real or imaginary. Even an object can be the focus of a good story, for example: "The Little Engine That Could."

People have been telling stories for thousands of years. Stories have the power to cross cultures, to touch our emotions, to share common meanings and to connect us in the universal human experience.

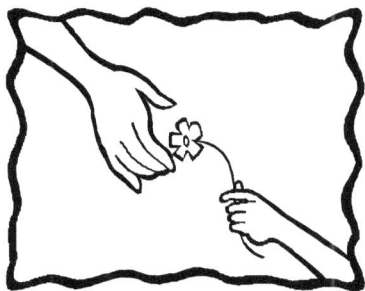

Have students brainstorm a list of spiritual virtues (patience, generosity, courtesy, love, justice, sacrifice, etc.). Write these on the board. Then ask each student to select one quality and to think of a story to illustrate it. Stories can be taken from the Bahá'í writings, from current events, from a history book, magazine, personal experience or any other source.

For example, to illustrate sacrifice, one might tell the story of Ashraf's mother (Gleanings from the Writings of Bahá'u'lláh: p. 134), of Dr. Shishman (God Passes By: p. 165-6), or accounts from the Dawnbreakers. Books about 'Abdu'l-Bahá contain many stories that illustrate spiritual virtues.

Students should come prepared to tell their story next time. They should stay within a 2-3 minute time limit. The talk should include a memorized quote about the virtue they have selected, in addition to memorable opening and closing lines.

9. ONE-MINUTE FEEDBACK

WORKSHOP # 7: Adding Impact

Materials: Handouts, feedback, examples of visual aids (#6), 3x5 cards.

NOTE: This workshop is approx. 2½ hours long

1. WELCOME AND PRAYERS (2 min.)

2. FEEDBACK AND REVIEW (8 min.)

a. What is the purpose of the opening and closing lines of a speech?

b. Why should Bahá'í teachers first teach their own selves?

c. In addition to public speaking skills, what qualities
are needed for an effective presentation of the Faith?

3. HOMEWORK CHECK: Virtue story (50 min.)

Appoint timekeeper and fill counter. Begin each talk with a speaker introduction and audience greeting. Share and critique the 2-3 minute virtues stories, which should include a memorized quote plus memorable opening and closing lines. Share timekeeper and fill counter reports.

4. ADDING IMPACT (5 min.)

You can liven up your speech and emphasize the main points through the use of music, poetry, drama, quotations, stories, questions, visual aids, gestures, sound effects or other techniques. But don't overdo it! One or two of these may be sufficient for a short talk.
A few examples are listed below. *(Have students read aloud.)*

> **A. Use questions to focus the audience's attention on your topic.**
> Example: "What if the earth were one country?"
>
> **B. Include quotable sentences that make an impact.**
> Example: "The earth is but one country, and mankind its citizens." [a]
> Example: "Ask not what your country can do for you.
>   Ask what you can do for your country." [b]
> Example: "Some say peace is impossible. We say peace is inevitable."
>
> **C. Illustrate major points with stories.**
> Example: For race unity, the story of 'Abdu'l-Bahá and The Black Rose.
>
> **D. Include drama for added impact.**
> Example: Henry Ward Beecher began a speech against slavery
> by auctioning off a white slave girl with her hands tied behind her.
>
> **E. Use music to explain a concept.**
> Example: Play the notes of a chord to explain unity in diversity.

a. Bahá'u'lláh, *Gleanings,* p.250   b. John F. Kennedy

5. GESTURES (25 min.)

Gestures and facial expressions can make the speaker seem more relaxed and help the audience to better understand the ideas. Try these examples:

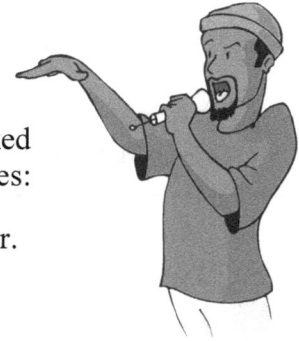

a. Use your hands to show size, shape, weight, direction or number.
b. Clasp your hands together to show unity.
c. Act out a scene from a story as you are telling it.
d. Hold up an index finger to indicate that there is only one God.
e. Flap your arms up and down like the wings of a bird to illustrate the equality of women and men; then show what happens when one wing is weaker than the other.

What gestures could be used with each sentence? →

- I can't eat another bite.
- It's freezing in here!
- Stop right there.
- Come on over.
- I don't know.

Be sure your gestures are large enough to be seen by everyone, but not so large that they distract from your speech. Practice with a friend or in front of a mirror until your movements look natural.

☐ Personal story with gestures

> Appoint timekeeper and fill counter. Have students come to the front and share a personal experience (30–60 seconds). They should begin with a greeting and, as they speak, include at least two gestures. Give them a few minutes to prepare. Ask for positive critiques, timekeeper and fill counter reports.

6. VISUAL AIDS (5 min.)

Visual aids can enhance a speech by allowing the audience to see what you are talking about. To illustrate the beauty of diversity, for example, you might show two garden pictures: one with identical flowers and the other with many-colored flowers. Visual aids should be large enough for all to see. If you are pointing to a chart, poster, map or other object, be sure to stand to the side so the audience has a clear view. A few examples of visual aids are listed below.

Show these or any others that are available.

a. A map to show the exiles of Bahá'u'lláh
b. A photograph of each Bahá'í House of Worship
c. A graph to illustrate progress in giving to the local Fund
d. A felt lesson to explain the principle of progressive revelation
e. Candles to light when reciting the "Seven Candles of Unity" by 'Abdu'l-Bahá
f. Heavy chains to show how the prisoners were kept in the Síyáh-Chál
g. A veil to describe how Táhirih removed hers

7. THE POWER OF WORDS (55 min.)

Have students read aloud from their worksheets and do the exercises together as a class. Depending on the time available, you might complete the entire worksheet or select only certain items for students to work on during class. Two or three items may be sufficient for the younger students. More capable students can finish at home. The class can schedule an extra session if desired.

8. HOMEWORK: Speaker's choice

Ask students to prepare a two-minute speech on any topic of their choice. They should make the speech interesting by using music, poetry, drama, quotes, stories, vivid words, questions, visual aids, gestures, sound effects or other techniques. Remind them not to overdo it. The speech should also have strong opening and closing lines.

9. ONE-MINUTE FEEDBACK

THE POWER OF WORDS

> *The words you use have a major impact on the quality of your speech. Choose them carefully to express exactly what you want to say. Let's start with a few things to avoid.*

(1) DON'T APOLOGIZE: Even if true, avoid phrases like these:

- I'm really nervous.
- Please don't expect much.
- I'm not good at public speaking.
- I don't have a lot to say on this topic, but here goes…

By drawing attention to your shortcomings, you are asking the audience to focus on these rather than on what you have to say. Practice your relaxation techniques, greet the audience and begin your speech with confidence. Once you get started, your nerves will calm down.

(2) AVOID JARGON: Jargon is specialized vocabulary that is familiar to some groups but that sounds strange or confusing to others. Bahá'í vocabulary, for example, includes words such as: Manifestation, dispensation, progressive revelation, Center of the Covenant, Guardian, Naw-Rúz and Ayyám-i-Há. In a short speech, you might use one or two of these terms, but be sure to explain them if you do.

(3) AVOID INITIALS: It is not dignified to use the first letter of each word to refer to a Bahá'í institution, for example: LSA, RBC, UHJ. If you are giving a talk about one of these institutions, it is better to use the complete name, for example: "National Spiritual Assembly" instead of "NSA."

Re-write: ABM   ***Auxiliary Board Member***

---

(4) AVOID WORDINESS: A long, rambling speech may confuse or tire the audience and detract from your presentation. Short, concise sentences are easier to understand. Cut out the deadwood.

Wordy: It is important for every Bahá'í in the world to really make an effort to do everything in their power to regularly contribute to the Bahá'í Fund each and every month, and whether they have a lot of money or not, they should still give what they can, even if it's a small amount.

Re-write: Every Bahá'í, whether rich or poor, should contribute regularly to the Fund.

Wordy: Do you think there is anyone in the world, whether in heaven or on earth, who has the power and the ability to take away our problems and troubles, or any of the large or small challenges that life sends our way, or the difficulties that confront our families and friends, except for the supreme Creator of the universe?

Re-write: ***"Is there any remover of difficulties save God?"*** *(Bahá'í Prayers, p.28)*

---

(5) INCLUDE DETAILS: The more specific your words are, the better.

Too general: "I saw a plant." The word "plant" doesn't give the audience much of a picture. "Flower" would be more specific, and even better would be "rose." Additional details will give the audience a clearer image of what you mean.

plant > flower > rose > yellow rose > wilted yellow rose in a cracked crystal vase

Now you try it:

animal >

clothing >

(6) USE VIVID WORDS: Action words and descriptive adjectives will bring your speech to life.

Boring: We rode in his car.
Better: We bounced along in his old red clunker.

Re-write: Make these sentences sparkle with more vivid language:

The woman reached out her hand.

The picnic was nice, with good weather, good food and good friends.

(7) USE REPETITION: Repeating a phrase gives it added impact.

Example: I have a dream that one day…the sons of former slaves and the sons of former slave owners will be able to sit down together…I have a dream that my four little children will one day live in a nation where they will not be judged by the color of their skin…I have a dream that one day…little black boys and little black girls will be able to join hands with little white boys and white girls as sisters and brothers. I have a dream today. (Dr. Martin Luther King, Jr., 1963)

What phrase does Dr. King repeat, and what point is he trying to emphasize?

With the phrase "I have a dream…" he repeatedly reminds the audience that racial equality is still a dream and not yet a reality today.

(8) SENSORY LANGUAGE: The use of words that appeal to the senses (sight, hearing, taste, touch and smell) will add variety to your speech and give the audience a clearer understanding of what you mean.

Sight

Boring: The moonlight shone on the lake.
Better: The pale yellow moonlight shimmered on the windswept lake.
Brainstorm: What "sight" words could you use to describe:
- A fire... *(blazing, flickering, leaping orange flames, soft warm glow...)*
- Clouds...
- Snow falling...
- A kitten playing...

Re-write: They walked past some buildings.

Sound

Boring: He heard a noise.
Better: He heard a soft, rhythmic thumping sound coming from the attic.
Brainstorm: What "sound" words could you use to describe:
- A busy city street...
- A country meadow...
- A big Naw-Rúz party...
- A middle school concert...

Re-write: There was an interesting sound coming from his book bag.

Taste

Boring: For lunch they ate soup, salad and bread.
Better: For lunch they ate a bowl of creamy potato soup, with a crisp green salad and homemade wheat bread fresh from the oven.
Brainstorm some taste words: *(crisp, juicy, oily, salty, sour, chewy, mouth-watering...)*

Re-write: The medicine tasted bad.

Touch

Boring: We walked through the jungle.
Better: Hot and dripping with sweat, we dragged ourselves through the
   steamy jungle, a thousand insects biting our arms and legs.
Brainstorm some touch words: *(burning, freezing, leathery, sharp, smooth, velvety,*
   silky, creamy, like sandpaper, like rubbing fish scales the wrong way...)

Re-write: She reached into the mystery bag and felt something.

Smell

Boring: Breakfast smelled good.
Better: The bacon was sizzling, the orange juice was fresh-squeezed,
   and the smell of sweet sticky cinnamon buns wafted through the air.
Brainstorm some smell words: *(smoky, burnt, musty, perfumed, fresh paint,*
   baby-powder fresh, like a dead skunk, like rotten eggs)

Re-write: There was an interesting smell coming from the garage.

(9) EMPHASIS: There are different ways to read the following phrase from 'Abdu'l-Bahá.
If a particular word is stressed, this gives it greater significance. *(Bahá'í Prayers, p.204)*

***Ask students to read the following examples out loud
and to explain how the meaning changes with each one.***

(a) "**Unite** the hearts of Thy servants."
  (This one stresses the word unite, calling attention to the importance of unity.)

(b) "Unite the **hearts** of Thy servants."
  (This emphasizes hearts, as opposed to minds or actions.)

(c) "Unite the hearts of **Thy** servants."
  (This highlights the fact that we belong to God.)

(d) "Unite the hearts of Thy **servants**."
  (This stresses that we are His servants, not His partners.)

All of these meanings are true, but we can choose which one to emphasize.

(10) ALLITERATION: Alliteration occurs when two or more words in a phrase start with the same letter or sound. This repetition of sounds sets up a rhythm that is musical to the ear. It adds a poetic flavor and makes the passage more memorable. A familiar example of alliteration is the tongue twister, "Peter Piper picked a peck of pickled peppers."

Shoghi Effendi's writings are filled with alliteration, for example: "As the lights of liberty flicker and go out, as the din of discord grows louder and louder every day, as the fires of fanaticism flame with increasing fierceness…" (Advent of Divine Justice, p. 5)

In the Guardian's passage above, which words show alliteration?

> *L = lights, liberty, louder, louder*
>
> *D = din, discord, day*
>
> *F = flicker, fires, fanaticism, flame, fierceness*

Using alliteration, write a title for a Bahá'í talk on any subject.

Example: The Reality of Race Relations in America
Example: From Merchant, to Messenger, to Martyr: The Life of the Báb
Example: Every Bahá'í Should Fast: Fact or Fiction?

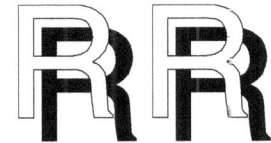

(11) PARALLEL STRUCTURE: This refers to phrases or sentences which are put together in a pattern, with repetition of key words and grammatical structures to produce a unified framework. Some examples are given below:

♥   ♥   ♥   ♥   ♥

"Blessed is the spot, and the house, and the place, and the city, and the heart…"
(Bahá'u'lláh, Bahá'í Prayers, title page)

"O Sufficer, I call on Thee, O Sufficer!
O Healer, I call on Thee, O Healer!
O Abider, I call on Thee, O Abider!"
(Bahá'u'lláh: Bahá'í Prayers, p. 97)

"Create in me a pure heart, O my God,
and renew a tranquil conscience within me, O my Hope!
Through the spirit of power confirm Thou me in Thy Cause, O my Best-Beloved…"
(Bahá'u'lláh: Prayers and Meditations, p. 248)

"To every thing there is a season, and a time to every purpose under the heaven:
A time to be born, and a time to die; A time to plant, and a time to reap;
A time to kill, and a time to heal; ...A time to mourn, and a time to dance;
A time to cast away stones, and a time to gather stones together...
A time to keep silence, and a time to speak..."
(Bible: Ecclesiastes, 3:1-7)

"First they came for the communists and I did not speak out...
Then they came for the socialists and I did not speak out...
Then they came for the labor leaders and I did not speak out...
Then they came for the Jews and I did not speak out...
Then they came for me, and there was no one left to speak out for me."
(Excerpts from Rev. Martin Niemoller who spent 7 years in a Nazi prison.)

Create a sentence using parallel structure with at least three items. Start with "Bahá'ís believe..."

> ***Bahá'ís believe there is only one God, only one religion, and only one human race.***

(12) COMPARISONS: By bringing two unrelated items together and suggesting similarities, a comparison allows us to see one in terms of the other. This new perspective gives us a deeper understanding of the first item, and it adds clarity and freshness to our speech.

The Bahá'í writings are filled with comparisons. For example, people are often compared to the flowers of a garden. Of course, people aren't really flowers, but the comparison helps us to understand the beauty of different skin colors, just as we already recognize the beauty of the different colored flowers in a garden.

A comparison can use the words "like" or "as," for example: ***"Mullá Husayn was like a lion in battle."*** The comparison can also be direct, without using "like" or "as," for example: ***"He was a lion in battle."*** Either way, the listener understands that Mullá Husayn showed the qualities of a lion: courage, strength and skill. In the passages below, what two items are being compared and how does the comparison add to our understanding?

"Bahá'u'lláh...'compared the coloured people* to the black pupil of the eye', through which 'the light of the spirit shineth forth'." *(Shoghi Effendi: Lights of Guidance, p. 526)*

"Although the pupil of the eye is black, it is the source of light."
('Abdu'l-Bahá: Compilation on Women, p. 361)

"O thou who hast an illumined heart! Thou art even as the pupil of the eye, the very wellspring of the light, for God's love hath cast its rays upon thine inmost being and thou hast turned thy face toward the Kingdom of thy Lord." *('Abdu'l-Bahá: Selections, p. 113)*

"Thou art dark in countenance and bright in character. Thou art like unto the pupil of the eye which is dark in colour, yet it is the fount of light and the revealer of the contingent world." *('Abdu'l-Bahá: Selections, p. 114)*

* Note: This term was in common usage when the passage was translated decades ago.

Can you think of other comparisons in the Bahá'í writings?

- *God's Prophets are compared to perfect mirrors, reflecting the rays of one sun.*
- *The Prophets are also compared to teachers at different grade-levels in a school.*
- *People are compared to the waves of one sea and the leaves of one tree.*
- *Bahá'í marriage is compared to a fortress.*
- *The fund is the "life blood" of the Cause.*
- *The whole world is worth as much as the black in the eye of a dead ant.*

An over-used comparison is called a "cliché." *Red as a rose, fresh as a daisy, hard as a rock, cold as ice, quiet as a mouse:* these probably sounded charming the first time they were used, but they have since lost their appeal, and now sound tired and worn out.

Re-write using an original comparison:

Quiet as a mouse…

Quiet as a snowflake falling in a meadow at midnight…
Quiet as a hungry baby in wet diapers at 3 a.m.…

Now try these:

His heart was as hard as…

They were as friendly as…

She jumped like…

The wind blew like…

Write a direct comparison, without using "like" or "as."

Bahá'í administration is…

There are many other ways to increase the power of your words.
The exercises on this worksheet will give you a good start.

WORKSHOP # 8: Microphones and Media

Materials: Handouts, feedback, hand-held microphone with floor stand and amplifier, copies of "The Vision of Race Unity" for each student, clip-on mike, 3x5 cards. (If real equipment is not available, simulate using household objects.)

NOTE: This workshop is approx. 2½ hours long.

1. WELCOME AND PRAYERS (2 min.)

2. FEEDBACK AND REVIEW (8 min.)

a. What are some of the ways to add impact to a speech? ⟶

> Music, poetry, drama, quotes, stories, questions, visual aids, gestures, sound effects, vivid action words, repetition, sensory details, alliteration, parallel structure, comparisons

b. What are these and why should we avoid them?

- Apologies
- Abbreviations
- Jargon
- Wordiness

3. HOMEWORK CHECK: Two-minute talk on speaker's choice of topic (40 min.)

Appoint timekeeper, fill counter and introducers. Begin with greetings and share two-minute speeches on various topics. Look for techniques to add impact and strong opening and closing lines. End with critiques. The audience should be able to identify the purpose of each speech. Share timekeeper and fill counter reports.

4. USING A MICROPHONE (20 min.)

Have students introduce themselves using a floor mike. First show them:

- [ ] Where to position the mike in front of the audience *(not too far away)*
- [ ] How to adjust the height and angle of the mike
- [ ] How to turn the mike on and off
- [ ] How to remove and replace the mike in its holder
- [ ] How close to stand *(about the width of a large hand)*
- [ ] How to avoid tripping on the cord
- [ ] How to reduce feedback and adjust the volume
- [ ] Introduce self using a microphone

> If real equipment is not available, students can still practice most of these skills using simulated equipment. Give everyone a chance to practice. The same basic principles should apply: dignified walk, good posture, clear voice, three-second frame.

Note: To reduce feedback, be sure the mike is not too close to the amplifier or it could cause interference. In addition, with a portable sound system, place the amplifier between the microphone and the audience, i.e. stay behind the amplifier. Otherwise, the sound will travel from the mike to the amplifier and back through the mike, creating a feedback loop and producing an unpleasant screeching sound. (See diagram below.) With a permanently installed system, you should be able to place the mike anywhere.

Wrong amplifier placement   Correct amplifier placement

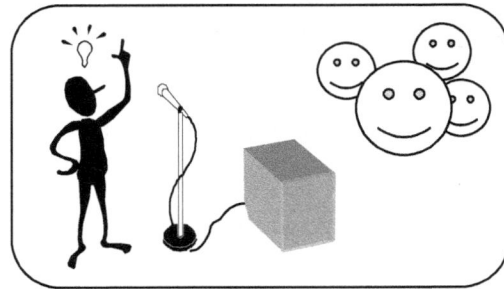

5. MEDIA INTERVIEWS (15 min.)

As the Faith grows, Bahá'ís will be increasingly asked for interviews by the media. For example, a newspaper reporter may attend a race unity event, and wish to speak with the organizers. A local radio station could interview a Bahá'í returning from a year of service overseas. A television station might run a story about the junior youth spiritual empowerment program, or explore how different religious groups celebrate the New Year.

Media interviews present both an opportunity and a challenge. We have an opportunity to share the Bahá'í teachings with thousands of people at once, but not always under favorable conditions. Some reporters may be antagonistic to the Faith and try to present it in a bad light. Accuracy is also an issue. We have no final control over what actually goes into print or is broadcast over the air. However, we can prepare, pray and do the best that we can.

Remember that all media interviews dealing with the Faith should first be cleared with the Local Spiritual Assembly or other appropriate Bahá'í Institution.

See Appendix E for ways to approach local media outlets for a Bahá'í publicity campaign.

See Appendix F for ways to respond to controversy.

☐ Guidelines for Media Interviews

Read handout with students and check for understanding.

6. INTERVIEW PRACTICE (60 min.)

Working in pairs, each student will conduct a media interview. They should take turns acting as the reporter. Each interview should last three minutes maximum. The reporter should prepare three questions and share them with the guest in advance. An additional spontaneous question will be generated from the audience at the time of the interview. Using their worksheets, students should determine:

- The Medium (newspaper, radio or TV)
- The Format (phone interview, talk show, live news, press conference…)
- The Tone (is the reporter friendly, hostile or neutral?)
- The Topic
- Three prepared questions

Sample Interview

Good afternoon viewers. I'm Victor Deerslayer from TV Channel 19. We are here on the steps of the courthouse with live coverage of the "Smith vs. State" adoption trial. My guest is Jennifer Smith, wife of the couple that was just denied adoption of a child of another race. The Smiths are purple and the child is pink.

Question 1:   Mrs. Smith, how do you feel about the verdict?
Question 2:   Why would a **purple** family want to adopt a **pink** child?
Question 3:   Did your religious faith play any part in your decision?
Audience: Why should a child suffer just so you can prove your point?

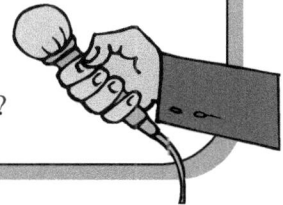

Give students twenty minutes to prepare. Appoint timekeeper and fill counter. Use a hand-held mike for the reporter or clip-on mike for the guest. Present each interview (including the audience question) in front of the class. After two minutes, have the timekeeper call "One minute left!" and at three minutes, have the timer count down with fingers "5 – 4 – 3 – 2 – 1 – Time!" and end the interview—even if not finished. This will help prepare students for the reality of a busy reporter with a deadline. Follow with brief critiques and a fill counter report.

7. HOMEWORK: "Vision of Race Unity" summary

Provide each student with a copy of "The Vision of Race Unity," a statement by the National Assembly of the U.S. Ask them to read the document at home with adult help if necessary. If more suitable for the needs of your community, select a different document, e.g. "Two Wings of a Bird" by the U.S. National Assembly, or "The Promise of World Peace" by the Universal House of Justice. Writing on their worksheets, students should identify the title, author and date; determine the audience (i.e. who the message was written to); give a brief summary with key points; select a quote from the document; and prepare a visual aid. See examples on following page.

8. ONE-MINUTE FEEDBACK

WRITTEN BY A 12-YEAR OLD

Title: The Vision of Race Unity
Author: NSA of the Bahá'ís of the US
Publication Date: 1991
Audience: Every American

Summary: This book is about the unity of the races. Bahá'ís believe that the oneness of mankind is necessary for a peaceful world. In fact, the Bahá'í Faith revolves around race unity. It is our main purpose of being on earth. The solution to racial and ethnic conflict is the oneness of mankind. The responsibility for race unity rests on both black and white Americans eliminating their prejudice and trying to be unified.

WRITTEN BY A 17-YEAR OLD

Title: The Vision of Race Unity
Author: NSA of the Bahá'ís of the US
Publication Date: 1991
Audience: Every American

Summary: Racial prejudice is America's most challenging issue. The oneness of humanity is the central teaching of the Bahá'í Faith and the goal of human existence on this planet. To reach this goal, we will have to make many changes in our society. Our peace and prosperity depend on it. If we don't change, we will face many dangers. The key is fellowship between Black and White. Both are responsible. Education is the fastest way to achieve this goal. We offer the example of the Bahá'í community as a model.

WORKSHOP # 9: Official Presentations

Materials: Handouts, feedback, self-assessment form from workshops #1 and #5, course evaluation forms, 3x5 cards. If possible, enlist the help of someone who can translate into another language (#5).

NOTE: This workshop is approx. 2½ hours long

1. WELCOME AND PRAYERS (2 min.)

2. FEEDBACK AND REVIEW (8 min.)

a. Things to remember when using a microphone?
b. Guidelines for media interviews?
c. How are media interviews both a challenge and an opportunity?

3. HOMEWORK CHECK: "Vision of Race Unity" summary (25 min.)

Each student should have read "The Vision of Race Unity" and completed the summary sheet. Review their answers, discuss the main points in the document, then share their quotes and visual aids. Students should keep their papers for use with the next exercise.

4. PRESENTATION TO LOCAL OFFICIALS (45 min.)

Students will practice making formal presentations to local officials such as the mayor, city council or school board.

Remember that permission from the Assembly may be required beforehand. A sample letter of introduction from the Assembly is included in Appendix G.

Students should begin by greeting the audience and introducing themselves and the Bahá'í community. See sample at right.

Sample Presentation

(Students line up facing the Mayor)

ELENA: Good morning Mayor Jones and Council members. My name is Elena. Our Bahá'í youth group would like to make a short presentation.

*(Students introduce themselves one by one.
Then two students step forward with the Race Unity booklet.)*

GUS: On behalf of the Bahá'í community of Springfield, we would like to present you with this booklet, "The Vision of Race Unity."

(Show booklet.)

MINA: It talks about the elimination of racial prejudice and how we can establish unity between people of all colors and backgrounds.

GUS: Ming Li drew this picture to show what race unity means to her. And Jordan would like to share an excerpt from the booklet.

(Ming Li holds up her picture. Then Jordan steps forward, recites a short memorized passage, and steps back.)

MINA: This booklet was written by the National Spiritual Assembly of the Bahá'ís of the United States, and it is being presented to leaders of thought around the country. We hope you enjoy reading it.

(Gus presents booklet to Mayor.)

For the actual presentation, designate one person to answer any questions, and remember to bring a camera to record the event.

☐ Practice making a formal presentation

FRIENDS

> Divide students into teams to practice the presentation. Each team should have at least four people: two booklet presenters, one person to recite a quote and another to share a visual aid. Let students decide who does what, but make sure everyone has a part. They should use their own words, with the sample presentation serving only as a guide. Give them about fifteen minutes to practice. Then have each team present, followed by a positive critique.

5. SPEAKING THROUGH AN INTERPRETER (35 min.)

When making a presentation to a group that speaks a different language, you may have to speak through someone who can translate your words. This person is called an interpreter. By following a few simple rules, the experience will go a lot more smoothly and communication will be improved.

a. Do not speak louder than usual. The audience is not hard of hearing.
b. Look directly at the group or individual you are speaking to, not at the translator.
c. Speak slowly and clearly, using short sentences.
d. Stop after every sentence to allow for the translation.
e. Pay attention to your tone of voice. People will relate to your voice even if they do not understand the words.
f. Remember that the presentation will take twice the amount of time.

☐ Practice speaking through an interpreter

If there are speakers of other languages in the community, enlist their help with this exercise. Appoint timekeeper and fill counter. One by one, have each student face the audience, begin with a greeting, and give a one-minute impromptu talk on the Faith (including translation). Remind them to stop for translation after each sentence. The teacher should demonstrate first. If no speakers of other languages are available, the "translation" can be done by having someone paraphrase each sentence in English. Follow with positive critiques. Share timekeeper and fill counter reports.

6. TIPS FOR PUBLIC SPEAKERS (15 min.) ✓

Go over this handout with students as a final course review.

7. ONE-MINUTE FEEDBACK

8. SELF-ASSESSMENT (10 min.)

Re-distribute the assessment forms. Have students complete the form for the "last day" using a red pen. Collect the forms and later compare their progress from the beginning to the end of the course. You may wish to tabulate the results and select a few of their written comments to share with the community. The assessments can then be returned to the students to file with their course handouts.

9. COURSE EVALUATION (10 min.)

Have students complete an evaluation of the course (see handouts). Collect and use the information to improve the next course.

10. CLOSING

Congratulate students on completing the course. Make arrangements for a special ceremony to present each student with a certificate of completion (at end of student handout section). The class may wish to help with the planning for this event. Remember to consult with the local Assembly to arrange future speaking opportunities for your students. Good luck!

Some students may want to continue developing their speaking skills after the course has ended. You might suggest that they join Toastmasters if there is a local club. Toastmasters is an international, non-profit, volunteer organization dedicated to improving public speaking skills. Their weekly meetings provide many opportunities for practice, and for teaching the Faith as well. Look for local listings in the community calendar section of the newspaper, call (800) 993-7732, or find them on the Internet at < www.toastmasters.com >.

"...In God's sight,
the best of all ways to worship Him
is to educate the children and train them
in all the perfections of humankind;
and no nobler deed than this
can be imagined."

(Selections from the Writings of 'Abdu'l-Bahá, p. 139)

Bahá'í Public Speaking

STUDENT HANDOUTS

As a convenience for those who have purchased this book, student handouts are also available for downloading from: www.UnityWorksStore.com under the "workshops" menu.

(c) UnityWorks LLC. Permission is granted for one classroom teacher to copy these handouts for their own students as needed. The copyright information must clearly show on all copies.

WORKSHOP # 1: Beginning Exercises

WORKSHOP GOALS: You will learn to…

a. Stand up with courage in front of a group
b. Speak with a strong clear voice
c. Use good posture and eye contact
d. Read aloud well
e. Memorize Bahá'í passages
f. Answer questions about the Faith
g. Research a topic from the Writings
h. Write a speech
i. Give a short prepared talk
j. Give a short impromptu talk
k. Introduce another speaker
l. Present Bahá'í materials to local officials
m. Speak through an interpreter
n. Use a microphone
o. Be interviewed by the media

ASSIGNMENT:

☐ Choose a partner to practice with outside of class: _____

☐ Schedule a time to practice: _____
(For example, call or meet your partner every Sunday at 4 p.m.)

BEGINNING EXERCISES

☐ Walk to the front and back in a relaxed, dignified manner

☐ Stand facing the audience with good posture and eye contact for 3 seconds

☐ Introduce yourself (name, age, town)

☐ Introduce another speaker

TONE OF VOICE:

● I'm really angry.　　● I'm really sad.　　● I'm really embarrassed.　　● I'm really happy.

HOMEWORK: Watch a TV news show for about 10 minutes.

a. Listen to each announcer's tone of voice.
b. Watch their lip and mouth movements.
c. Can you understand each word?
d. Pay attention to pauses.
e. Where are their eyes looking?
f. Observe their posture and facial expressions.
g. Describe their hair and clothing.
h. Take notes and be ready to share what you have learned next time.

Sharing the Beauty of God

by Diedre Merrill and Gayle Woolson

The room was filled with over 100 people. My friend had just completed a perfect performance on his violin. The applause of the audience sounded like thunder in my ears. Now, it was my turn.

I tried hard to concentrate on the opening sentence of my speech. I knew that once I got started, the rest of the speech would follow easily. I had practiced it so many times with my partner. I felt like a race horse, well trained and eager to start. My heart pounded in my chest. I thought of my partner reminding me to speak slowly. I must not race through my speech like a runaway stallion.

I love the words of Bahá'u'lláh. I love the way I feel when I recite them from memory. When I first looked at my speech, there were words I did not know. But my partner explained the meaning of them to me. He said the words of Bahá'u'lláh are very powerful and overflowing with wisdom. They have an effect upon the hearts of those who hear them. Now was my chance to share these words.

If I said them too fast, it would be like throwing a bucket of water at someone who was thirsty. It would quickly run off onto the floor, doing little good. If I took care to speak slowly and clearly, Bahá'u'lláh's words would have time to trickle over those in the audience with their life-giving energy.

"THE GREAT MISSION OF CHILDREN." The words exploded in my ears--the title of my speech. The eyes of my partner were filled with love as he introduced me. He was confident that I would say my speech perfectly, as I had so many times. I wanted to do my very best.

My partner told me that children like you and me, who are living in the world today, have a destiny before God. We have a very important job. We are expected to make the whole world like a single neighborhood.

'Abdu'l-Bahá said, "Love is the brightness of the beauty of God." It is up to us to share that love with everyone.

I walked to the microphone. Slowly, I began my speech. "Humanity has entered into a glorious new universal age…" Everything was going well. I saw other children in the audience. I looked at them as I continued. "We children are very fortunate to be living in this wonderful age and we have an important role to play in helping establish peace and understanding among the people of all religions, races, nations and classes."

Their eyes seemed to twinkle with excitement. Maybe they were asking, "How can we do this?" 'Abdu'l-Bahá indicated one way when He said, "Encourage ye the school children, from their earliest years, to deliver speeches of high quality." A warm feeling poured over me. I was doing just what 'Abdu'l-Bahá wanted.

I continued my speech. I was talking about the path of life that leads us towards achieving a wonderful future. I could see the wonder in people's faces as they imagined what such a future would be like. The answer was in my speech, so I hurried on.

"A magnificent view of the future is described in the Bahá'í Writings: 'the earth will be transformed; …cooperation and union will be established; …the human race will be like one family.'" I pictured my family, my brothers and sisters, my aunts and uncles. The picture kept growing larger and larger until it included everyone in the world.

Too quickly my speech was over. From the light shining from the faces of my partner and the others in the audience, I knew I had done well. I had shared the "brightness of the beauty of God."

(c) 1993, National Spiritual Assembly of the Bahá'ís of the United States. From Brilliant Star Magazine. Used with permission.

Self Assessment

Date: _____ (first day of course) → Use pencil
Date: _____ (halfway through course) → Use blue pen
Date: _____ (last day of course) → Use red pen

Name: _____ Teacher: _____

(1) How comfortable do you feel? (Circle one number for each item)	Very Un- comfortable		In the Middle		Very Comfortable
a. Standing in front of a group	1	2	3	4	5
b. Speaking with a strong clear voice	1	2	3	4	5
c. Using good posture and eye contact	1	2	3	4	5
d. Reading aloud	1	2	3	4	5
e. Memorizing Bahá'í passages	1	2	3	4	5
f. Answering questions about the Faith	1	2	3	4	5
g. Researching a topic from the Writings	1	2	3	4	5
h. Writing a speech	1	2	3	4	5
i. Giving a short prepared talk	1	2	3	4	5
j. Giving a short impromptu talk	1	2	3	4	5
k. Introducing another speaker	1	2	3	4	5
l. Presenting items to community leaders	1	2	3	4	5
m. Speaking through an interpreter	1	2	3	4	5
n. Using a microphone	1	2	3	4	5
o. Being interviewed by the media	1	2	3	4	5

(2) Connect the circles.

(3) Tell me about yourself as a public speaker. (Use back of page)

Self Assessment, page 2

First day of course:

Halfway through course:

Last day of course:

WORKSHOP # 2: Speaking Style

REVIEW: Teaching, workshop goals, proper attitude, presentation skills, three-second frame

SHARE HOMEWORK: Observations from TV newscast

EXERCISES

☐ Relaxation techniques: shake, stretch, deep breaths, pray

☐ State name with 3-second frame: bad posture / good posture

☐ Sentence A: weak voice / strong voice

☐ Sentence B: with a big ego / with an attitude of service

☐ Sentence C: mumbled words / clearly pronounced words

☐ Sentence D: eyes down / good eye contact

☐ Sentence E: monotone / melodious voice

☐ Sentence F: too fast / too slow / just right

Sentences for Practice Exercises

A. Good evening friends. Welcome to our Holy Day celebration.
B. Our community is pleased to present the Bahá'í Youth Workshop.
C. The Youth Workshop is a group of young Bahá'ís who are sharing a message of unity through their music and dance.
D. Unity is one of the most important teachings of the Baha'i Faith.
E. After the performance, we invite you to stay for refreshments and we will be glad to answer any questions you might have.
F. And now, the Bahá'í Youth Workshop.

CHARACTERISTICS OF A GOOD PUBLIC SPEAKER (take notes)

DISCUSSION: How does the speaker's presentation style (voice, posture, eye contact, etc.) affect the audience? How does it affect the speaker?

MEMORIZATION ──────────➤

HOMEWORK:
Select one of the quotations from the back of this handout to memorize for the next class.

"Now is the time to speak forth
and to deliver speeches,
the time to teach and to give testimony.
Loosen thy tongue...
The Holy Spirit speaketh
through the innermost essence
of the human tongue..."

('Abdu'l-Bahá)

QUOTATIONS ON SPEECH

Select one or more of the following quotations to memorize. Look up the meaning of any words you don't know. Practice with your partner and be ready to recite next time. Use good posture, eye contact, voice control and a three-second frame.

(1) "This is the day in which to speak…Within every word a new spirit is hidden." *(Bahá'u'lláh: quoted in Advent of Divine Justice, p. 69)*

(2) "We have ordained that complete victory should be achieved through speech and utterance…" *(Bahá'u'lláh: Tablets of Bahá'u'lláh, p. 197-198)*

(3) "Encourage ye the school children, from their earliest years, to deliver speeches of high quality…" *('Abdu'l-Bahá: Selections, p. 134)*

(4) "It is the hope of 'Abdu'l-Bahá that those youthful souls…even as a nightingale endowed with speech, will cry out the secrets of the Heavenly Realm." *('Abdu'l-Bahá: Selections, p. 134)*

(5) "Grant, O my God, that I may not be reckoned among those whose ears are deaf, whose eyes are blind, whose tongues are speechless and whose hearts have failed to comprehend." *(Selections from the Báb, p. 216)*

(6) "Whoso openeth his lips in this day, and maketh mention of the name of his Lord, the hosts of Divine inspiration shall descend upon him from the heaven of My name, the All-Knowing, the All-Wise. On him shall also descend the Concourse on high, each bearing aloft a chalice of pure light." *(Bahá'u'lláh: quoted in Advent of Divine Justice, p. 71)*

(7) "From the texts of the wondrous, heavenly Scriptures they should memorize phrases and passages…so that in the course of their speech they may recite divine verses whenever the occasion demandeth it, inasmuch as these holy verses are the most potent elixir, the greatest and mightiest talisman. So potent is their influence that the hearer will have no cause for vacillation." *(Bahá'u'lláh: Tablets of Bahá'u'lláh, p. 200)*

(8) "It is my earnest hope that you…may be so enkindled by the flame set ablaze by the hand of God as to illumine the whole world through the quickening energy of the love of God, and that through the eloquence of your speech, the fluency of your tongue, and the confirmations of the Holy Spirit you will be empowered to expound divine wisdom in such manner that men of eloquence, and the scholars and sages of the world, will be lost in bewilderment." *(Shoghi Effendi: Bahiyyih Khanum, p. 100)*

WORKSHOP # 3: Basic Presentations

REVIEW

a. List several ways to relax before giving a talk.
b. Name some elements of speech and explain why each is important.

SHARE HOMEWORK: Memorized quotations

Remember good posture, eye contact, voice control and three-second frame.

EXERCISES

☐ Give a one-minute talk on "What is the Bahá'í Faith?"

☐ Draw a "pictoscript"

☐ Library book presentation

☐ Mini-interview with the librarian

LIBRARY BOOK PRESENTATION

- *On behalf of the Bahá'í community, we would like to present this children's book to the library.*

- *The book (El Regalo) is about animals who are always fighting because they follow different religious teachings.*

- *Then a dove brings them a new book and they learn to live together in peace.*

Librarian: "Thank you so much for this beautiful book! I've heard of the Bahá'í Faith before but don't really know much about it. Can you tell me something about Bahá'í?"

HOMEWORK: Prepare a one-minute talk on the Bahá'í principle of race unity. Include a short memorized quote from the Writings. Do not memorize your talk. You may use a pictoscript or keywords on 3x5 cards if desired. Practice with your partner and in front of a mirror.

WORKSHOP # 4: Answering Questions

REVIEW

a. Backwards buildup
b. Pictoscript

SHARE HOMEWORK: One-minute speech on race unity

Remember good posture, eye contact, voice control and 3-second frame

☐ Greet the audience
☐ Introduce the speaker
☐ One-minute prepared talk on race unity

Positive critique notes on my talk:

Areas for improvement:

ANSWERING QUESTIONS

☐ Prepared response (list A or B)
☐ Impromptu response (list C)

HOMEWORK

Choose a topic and prepare a two-minute speech for a Bahá'í fireside. The topic should be one that you feel strongly about and can talk about with sincerity, enthusiasm and conviction. Research the topic and write key words or draw a pictoscript on 3x5 cards. You may use one or more ideas per card. Memorize at least one quote on the topic, without memorizing the speech itself. Be prepared to give the speech next time.

| -1- Progressive Revelation | -2- Names of Prophets | -3- Like sun in mirror | -4- Like teachers in school |

WORKSHOP # 5: Organizing a Speech

REVIEW

a. Prepared vs. impromptu talks:

b. Ways to prepare for a talk:

c. Examples of an audience greeting and why it's helpful:

d. Information to include when introducing a speaker:

SHARE HOMEWORK: Two-minute fireside talk

Positive critique notes on my talk:

Areas for improvement:

PURPOSE OF A SPEECH

Every speech should be planned with the end result in mind. Ask yourself: Why am I giving this speech? What is the topic and why is it important to me?

You must also think about your topic from the audience's point of view. Why is the topic important to them? How does it affect their family, their neighborhood or community? How can you present your ideas so the audience will clearly understand your point of view?

What do you want the audience to do as a result of hearing your speech? Do you want them to attend a fireside? Host a Feast? Contribute to the Fund? Plan a devotional meeting? Organize a service project?

Are you trying to inform? Persuade? Inspire? Entertain? Be specific. Recommend solutions. Issue a call to action. Don't just let your speech begin and end in words.

MATCHING EXERCISE: Match each excerpt with the correct purpose of that speech.

Excerpt	Purpose of Presentation
(1) We hope you enjoyed our talent show. Thank you for coming.	___ INFORM
(2) On behalf of the Bahá'í community, we would like to present you with this booklet on race unity.	___ PERSUADE
(3) This story shows how, even with no money, just a few sincere Bahá'ís can achieve great victories for the Faith.	___ CALL TO ACTION
(4) We already know that the most effective way to teach is through personal firesides. So let's give it a try!	___ INSPIRE
(5) We need everyone to sign up for the service project this weekend.	___ ENTERTAIN

ORGANIZING A SPEECH

Once you have selected a topic and decided on the purpose of your speech, you will need to organize your ideas. Good organization is one key to an effective speech. When planning a car trip, it is important to bring a road map and to mark your destination with points of interest along the route. Every speech should have a road map as well. The audience needs to know where they are going and how they will get there, or they may become lost and confused. There are many ways to organize a speech. One way is to divide the speech into three parts: a beginning, middle and end.

- **The beginning section introduces the topic.** It tells the audience what the speech will be about and the main points you plan to cover. Using the car trip analogy, this is like saying: We are driving to the Bahá'í House of Worship and we will pass Kansas City, St. Louis and Chicago along the way.

- **The middle section is the main body of the speech.** It should include two or three main points. For each point, you should provide facts, examples, stories or quotes to support your views. The body of the speech should follow some kind of order (logical, chronological, cause and effect, comparison and contrast, etc.) This is like a road map for the audience.

- **The final section should summarize what the speech was about.** It can include your recommendations and a call to action. This is like the destination of the car trip.

To summarize: Tell them what you will say, say it, then tell them what you said.
Two examples are included below.

> Beginning: Welcome to our final class on becoming a Bahá'í. This morning we will review the basic Bahá'í teachings, the three Central Figures of the Faith, some laws and the Administrative Order. These are the essential elements of Bahá'í belief.
>
> Middle: Let's start with the basic teachings. The first teaching is... (etc.)
>
> End: That completes the class on becoming a Bahá'í. We reviewed the basic Bahá'í teachings, the three Central Figures of the Faith, some laws and the Administrative Order. We are delighted that you have all accepted these essential elements of Bahá'í belief, and have decided to join the Bahá'í Faith. Welcome!

> Beginning: This evening, I will share the Bahá'í teaching on progressive revelation. We will learn that God never leaves mankind alone. In every age, He sends us Prophets to teach us how to live together and to worship Him.
>
> Middle: A new Prophet comes every 500-1,000 years. Each one gives us a little more knowledge, just like teachers in a school. The first Prophet I will speak about is Abraham. Abraham was like the teacher for first grade. He taught that ...(etc.)
>
> End: That's how God talks to humanity. He never leaves us alone. He sends His Prophets to teach us how to live together and to worship Him. Just like teachers in a school, each one brings us something new. Bahá'ís call this progressive revelation. Are there any questions?

EXERCISES

A. Put sentences in logical order.
(Put a #1 by the sentence that should go first, etc.)

[ ] You will need flour, sugar, butter, oatmeal and raisins.
[ ] After mixing ingredients, spoon dough onto cookie sheet.
[ ] Before making the dough, pre-heat oven to 350 degrees.
[ ] Bake for 12 minutes; let cool and enjoy.
[ ] To bake Ayyám-i-Há cookies, first assemble the ingredients.

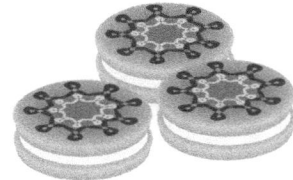

B. Put sentences in chronological order.

[ ] Bahá'u'lláh is God's most recent Messenger, declaring his mission in 1863.
[ ] The Jewish Holy Book is called the Torah.
[ ] The Hindu faith began in India with Krishna about 2,000 years before Christ.
[ ] Christianity began with the birth of Jesus about the year 1 A.D.
[ ] Next came Moses and the Jewish faith at around 1,300 BC in Egypt

C. Add beginning and ending sections to the middle paragraph below.

<u>Beginning:</u>

<u>Middle:</u> The devotional part of the Feast consists of prayers and readings from the Holy Writings. These can be chanted or set to music if desired. The business portion of the Feast provides time for the Bahá'í community to consult on matters of interest, to hear reports and to offer recommendations to the Local Spiritual Assembly. The social portion of Feast is the time when the believers can enjoy refreshments and fellowship, associating with each other in a spirit of love and unity.

<u>Ending:</u>

HOMEWORK: Re-write your fireside speech (or choose a new topic). First decide on the purpose of your speech and your own point of view. Then determine the audience's interest. Organize the speech with a beginning, middle and ending. Include two or three main points with the facts, examples, stories or quotes to support your views. Include an appeal to action at the end. Use the sample outline below as a guide. Make notes using keywords or pictures on 3x5 cards. Time your speech. It should be approximately **three minutes** long. Practice in front of a mirror and with your partner. Be ready for the next class. Good luck!

Sample outline for a speech

A. Beginning
  1. Attract audience attention
  2. Introduce topic

B. Middle
  1. First point
     a. Fact or example
     b. Fact or example
  2. Second point
     a. Fact or example
     b. Fact or example
  3. Third point
     a. Fact or example
     b. Fact or example

C. Ending
  1. Summary and conclusion
  2. Call to action

WORKSHOP # 6: Touching the Hearts

REVIEW

a. What are some of the purposes of a speech?

b. How is organizing a speech like planning a road trip?

c. Explain one way to organize a speech.

d. What does each section contain?

SHARE HOMEWORK: Three-minute fireside talk

Positive critique notes on my talk:

Areas for improvement:

OPENINGS AND CLOSINGS

A good opening line should grab the audience's attention and identify the topic of the speech. The opening, *"Today I'm going to talk about prejudice,"* identifies the topic, but it isn't too exciting. A better opening might be, *"What if all the children in the world were born without prejudice?"* A catchy opening might consist of a question, a surprising statistic, a challenging statement, a memorable quote, a joke, a story, a colorful picture or graph.

A good closing should tie everything together and summarize the main points of the speech. It might relate back to the opening question and provide the answer. For example: *"What if all the children in the world were born without prejudice? They are!"* The closing might include a poem, a quotation or an appeal for action. One famous speech about freedom (by Patrick Henry in 1775) ended with the rousing exclamation, *"Give me liberty or give me death!"*

It is a good idea to memorize the opening and closing lines. This will increase your confidence and ensure a strong start and finish to your speech.

☐ Write memorable opening and closing lines for each topic below. Be creative!

Martyrdom of the Báb

Opening line:

Closing line:

Bahá'í Elections

Opening line:

Closing line:

The Bahá'í Fund

Opening line:

Closing line:

Equality of Women and Men

Opening line:

Closing line:

DIFFUSING THE DIVINE FRAGRANCES

To be successful in "diffusing the Divine fragrances" we need more than public speaking skills. We must also develop spiritual qualities, reliance on God and a radiant heart. The audience will hear the spirit of a talk more than the words. Before we speak, we must first teach our own selves.

(A) "Let them, at the very outset, 'teach their own selves, that their speech may attract the hearts of their hearers.'" *(Bahá'u'lláh: quoted in Advent of Divine Justice, p. 60)*

(B) "'Abdu'l-Bahá has stressed that when Bahá'ís deliver their speeches in gatherings, they are to do so in an attitude of utmost humility and self-abnegation." *(Kitáb-i-Aqdas: Notes, p. 236)*

(C) "The heavenly glad tidings must be delivered with the utmost dignity and magnanimity." *('Abdu'l-Bahá: Selections, p. 160)*

(D) "With hearts overflowing with the love of God, with souls gladdened by the heavenly glad-tidings, and with extreme humility and lowliness, let them speak out with eloquent speech, and praise and glorify the Great Lord..." *('Abdu'l-Bahá: Women, p. 396-397)*

(E) "The teacher, when teaching, must be himself fully enkindled, so that his utterance, like unto a flame of fire, may exert influence and consume the veil of self and passion. ...so that he may teach with the melody of the Concourse on high - otherwise his teaching will have no effect." *('Abdu'l-Bahá: Selections, p. 270)*

(F) "O thou maid-servant of God! Whenever thou art intending to deliver a speech, turn thy face toward the Kingdom of ABHA and, with a heart detached, begin to talk. The breaths of the Holy Spirit will assist thee." *(Tablets of 'Abdu'l-Bahá, vol. 2, 1930 printing, p. 246)*

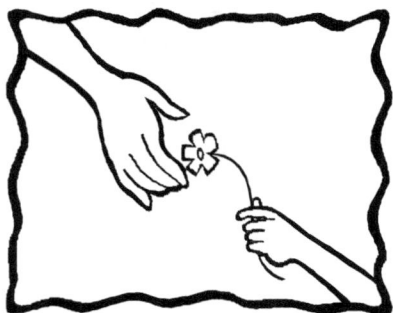

HOMEWORK: Another way to organize a speech is through the use of stories. Choose a spiritual virtue and think of a story to illustrate it. Stories can be taken from the Bahá'í writings, from current events, from a history book, magazine, personal experience or any other source. Come prepared to tell the story next time. Stay within a 2-3 minute time limit. Include a memorized quote about the virtue you have selected, and memorable opening and closing lines.

WORKSHOP # 7: Adding Impact

REVIEW

a. Purpose of opening and closing lines?
b. Why should Bahá'í teachers first teach their own selves?
c. Qualities needed for an effective presentation of the Faith?

SHARE HOMEWORK: Virtue stories (2-3 minutes each). Start with greeting.

Positive critique notes on my talk:

Areas for improvement:

ADDING IMPACT

You can liven up your speech and emphasize the main points through the use of music, poetry, drama, quotations, stories, questions, visual aids, gestures, sound effects or other techniques. But don't overdo it! One or two of these may be sufficient for a short talk. A few examples are listed below:

A. Use questions to focus the audience's attention on your topic.

Example: "What if the earth were one country?"

B. Include quotable sentences that make an impact.

Example: "The earth is one country, and mankind its citizens."

Example: "Ask not what your country can do for you.
Ask what you can do for your country."

Example: "Some say peace is impossible. We say peace is inevitable."

C. Illustrate major points with stories.

Example: For race unity, share the story of 'Abdu'l-Bahá and The Black Rose

D. Include drama for added impact.

Example: Henry Ward Beecher began a speech against slavery
by auctioning off a white slave girl with her hands tied behind her.

E. Use music to explain a concept.

Example: Play the notes of a chord to explain unity in diversity.

GESTURES

Gestures and facial expressions can make the speaker seem more relaxed and help the audience to better understand the ideas. Be sure your gestures are large enough to be seen by everyone, but not so large that they distract from your speech. Practice with a friend or in front of a mirror until your movements look natural.

☐ Personal story with gestures

VISUAL AIDS

Visual aids can enhance a speech by allowing the audience to see what you are talking about. To illustrate the beauty of diversity, for example, you might show two garden pictures: one with identical flowers and the other with many-colored flowers. Visual aids should be large enough for all to see. If you are pointing to a chart, poster, map or other object, be sure to stand to the side so the audience has a clear view. A few examples of visual aids are listed below:

- A map to show the exiles of Bahá'u'lláh
- A photograph of each Bahá'í House of Worship
- A graph to illustrate progress in giving to the local Fund
- A felt lesson to explain the principle of progressive revelation
- Candles to light when reciting the "Seven Candles of Unity" by 'Abdu'l-Bahá
- Heavy chains to show how the prisoners were kept in the Síyáh-Chál
- A veil to describe how Táhirih removed hers

THE POWER OF WORDS (see worksheet)

HOMEWORK: Speaker's choice

Prepare a two-minute speech on any topic of your choice. Make the speech interesting by using music, poetry, drama, quotes, stories, vivid words, questions, visual aids, gestures, sound effects or other techniques. The speech should have strong opening and closing lines.

THE POWER OF WORDS

> *The words you use have a major impact on the quality of your speech. Choose them carefully to express exactly what you want to say. Let's start with a few things to avoid.*

(1) DON'T APOLOGIZE: Even if true, avoid phrases like these:

- I'm really nervous.
- Please don't expect much.
- I'm not good at public speaking.
- I don't have a lot to say on this topic, but here goes…

By drawing attention to your shortcomings, you are asking the audience to focus on these rather than on what you have to say. Practice your relaxation techniques, greet the audience and begin your speech with confidence. Once you get started, your nerves will calm down.

(2) AVOID JARGON: Jargon is specialized vocabulary that is familiar to some groups but that sounds strange or confusing to others. Bahá'í vocabulary, for example, includes words such as: Manifestation, dispensation, progressive revelation, Center of the Covenant, Guardian, Naw-Rúz and Ayyám-i-Há. In a short speech, you might use one or two of these terms, but be sure to explain them if you do.

(3) AVOID INITIALS: It is not dignified to use the first letter of each word to refer to a Bahá'í institution, for example: LSA, RBC, UHJ. If you are giving a talk about one of these institutions, it is better to use the complete name, for example: "National Spiritual Assembly" instead of "NSA."

Re-write: ABM

(4) AVOID WORDINESS: A long, rambling speech may confuse or tire the audience and detract from your presentation. Short, concise sentences are easier to understand. Cut out the deadwood.

Wordy: It is important for every Bahá'í in the world to really make an effort to do everything in their power to regularly contribute to the Bahá'í Fund each and every month, and whether they have a lot of money or not, they should still give what they can, even if it's a small amount.

Re-write: Every Bahá'í, whether rich or poor, should contribute regularly to the Fund.

Wordy: Do you think there is anyone in the world, whether in heaven or on earth, who has the power and the ability to take away our problems and troubles, or any of the large or small challenges that life sends our way, or the difficulties that confront our families and friends, except for the supreme Creator of the universe?

Re-write:

(5) INCLUDE DETAILS: The more specific your words are, the better.

<u>Too general</u>: "I saw a plant." The word "plant" doesn't give the audience much of a picture. "Flower" would be more specific, and even better would be "rose." Additional details will give the audience a clearer image of what you mean.

plant > flower > rose > yellow rose > wilted yellow rose in a cracked crystal vase

Now you try it:

animal >

clothing >

(6) USE VIVID WORDS: Action words and descriptive adjectives will bring your speech to life.

<u>Boring</u>: We rode in his car.
<u>Better</u>: We bounced along in his old red clunker.

<u>Re-write</u>: Make these sentences sparkle with more vivid language:

The woman reached out her hand.

The picnic was nice, with good weather, good food and good friends.

(7) USE REPETITION: Repeating a phrase gives it added impact.

<u>Example</u>: I have a dream that one day…the sons of former slaves and the sons of former slave owners will be able to sit down together…I have a dream that my four little children will one day live in a nation where they will not be judged by the color of their skin…I have a dream that one day…little black boys and little black girls will be able to join hands with little white boys and white girls as sisters and brothers. I have a dream today. (Dr. Martin Luther King, Jr., 1963)

What phrase does Dr. King repeat, and what point is he trying to emphasize?

(8) SENSORY LANGUAGE: The use of words that appeal to the senses (sight, hearing, taste, touch and smell) will add variety to your speech and give the audience a clearer understanding of what you mean.

Sight

Boring: The moonlight shone on the lake.
Better: The pale yellow moonlight shimmered on the windswept lake.
Brainstorm: What "sight" words could you use to describe:
- A fire... *(blazing, flickering, leaping orange flames, soft warm glow...)*
- Clouds...
- Snow falling...
- A kitten playing...

Re-write: They walked past some buildings.

Sound

Boring: He heard a noise.
Better: He heard a soft, rhythmic thumping sound coming from the attic.
Brainstorm: What "sound" words could you use to describe:
- A busy city street...
- A country meadow...
- A big Naw-Rúz party...
- A middle school concert...

Re-write: There was an interesting sound coming from his book bag.

Taste

Boring: For lunch they ate soup, salad and bread.
Better: For lunch they ate a bowl of creamy potato soup, with a crisp green salad and homemade wheat bread fresh from the oven.
Brainstorm some taste words:

Re-write: The medicine tasted bad.

Touch

Boring: We walked through the jungle.
Better: Hot and dripping with sweat, we dragged ourselves through the
steamy jungle, a thousand insects biting our arms and legs.
Brainstorm some touch words:

Re-write: She reached into the mystery bag and felt something.

Smell

Boring: Breakfast smelled good.
Better: The bacon was sizzling, the orange juice was fresh-squeezed,
and the smell of sweet sticky cinnamon buns wafted through the air.
Brainstorm some smell words:

Re-write: There was an interesting smell coming from the garage.

(9) EMPHASIS: There are different ways to read the following phrase from 'Abdu'l-Bahá.
If a particular word is stressed, this gives it greater significance.

(a) "**Unite** the hearts of Thy servants."

(b) "Unite the **hearts** of Thy servants."

(c) "Unite the hearts of **Thy** servants."

(d) "Unite the hearts of Thy **servants**."

(10) ALLITERATION: Alliteration occurs when two or more words in a phrase start with the same letter or sound. This repetition of sounds sets up a rhythm that is musical to the ear. It adds a poetic flavor and makes the passage more memorable. A familiar example of alliteration is the tongue twister, "Peter Piper picked a peck of pickled peppers."

Shoghi Effendi's writings are filled with alliteration, for example: "As the lights of liberty flicker and go out, as the din of discord grows louder and louder every day, as the fires of fanaticism flame with increasing fierceness…" (Advent of Divine Justice, p. 5)

In the Guardian's passage above, which words show alliteration?

L =

D =

F =

Using alliteration, write a title for a Bahá'í talk on any subject.

Example: The Reality of Race Relations in America
Example: From Merchant, to Messenger, to Martyr: The Life of the Báb
Example: Every Bahá'í Should Fast: Fact or Fiction?

(11) PARALLEL STRUCTURE: This refers to phrases or sentences which are put together in a pattern, with repetition of key words and grammatical structures to produce a unified framework. Some examples are given below:

♥   ♥   ♥   ♥   ♥

"Blessed is the spot, and the house, and the place, and the city, and the heart…"
(Bahá'u'lláh, Bahá'í Prayers, title page)

"O Sufficer, I call on Thee, O Sufficer!
O Healer, I call on Thee, O Healer!
O Abider, I call on Thee, O Abider!"
(Bahá'u'lláh: Bahá'í Prayers, p. 97)

"Create in me a pure heart, O my God,
and renew a tranquil conscience within me, O my Hope!
Through the spirit of power confirm Thou me in Thy Cause, O my Best-Beloved…"
(Bahá'u'lláh: Prayers and Meditations, p. 248)

"To every thing there is a season, and a time to every purpose under the heaven:
A time to be born, and a time to die; A time to plant, and a time to reap;
A time to kill, and a time to heal; …A time to mourn, and a time to dance;
A time to cast away stones, and a time to gather stones together…
A time to keep silence, and a time to speak…"
(Bible: Ecclesiastes, Chapter 3)

"First they came for the communists and I did not speak out…
Then they came for the socialists and I did not speak out…
Then they came for the labor leaders and I did not speak out…
Then they came for the Jews and I did not speak out…
Then they came for me, and there was no one left to speak out for me."
(Excerpts from Rev. Martin Niemoller who spent 7 years in a Nazi prison.)

Create a sentence using parallel structure with at least three items. Start with, "Bahá'ís believe…"

(12) COMPARISONS: By bringing two unrelated items together and suggesting similarities, a comparison allows us to see one in terms of the other. This new perspective gives us a deeper understanding of the first item, and it adds clarity and freshness to our speech.

The Bahá'í writings are filled with comparisons. For example, people are often compared to the flowers of a garden. Of course, people aren't really flowers, but the comparison helps us to understand the beauty of different skin colors, just as we already recognize the beauty of the different colored flowers in a garden.

A comparison can use the words "like" or "as," for example: ***Mullá Husayn was like a lion in battle.*** The comparison can also be direct, without using "like" or "as," for example: ***He was a lion in battle.*** Either way, the listener understands that Mullá Husayn showed the qualities of a lion: courage, strength and skill. In the passages below, what two items are being compared and how does the comparison add to our understanding?

"Bahá'u'lláh…'compared the coloured people* to the black pupil of the eye', through which 'the light of the spirit shineth forth'." *(Shoghi Effendi: Lights of Guidance, p. 526)*

"Although the pupil of the eye is black, it is the source of light."
('Abdu'l-Bahá: Compilation on Women, p. 361)

"O thou who hast an illumined heart! Thou art even as the pupil of the eye, the very wellspring of the light, for God's love hath cast its rays upon thine inmost being and thou hast turned thy face toward the Kingdom of thy Lord." *('Abdu'l-Bahá: Selections, p. 113)*

"Thou art dark in countenance and bright in character. Thou art like unto the pupil of the eye which is dark in colour, yet it is the fount of light and the revealer of the contingent world." *('Abdu'l-Bahá: Selections, p. 114)*

* Note: This term was in common usage when the passage was translated decades ago.

Can you think of other comparisons in the Bahá'í writings?

An over-used comparison is called a "cliché." *Red as a rose, fresh as a daisy, hard as a rock, cold as ice, quiet as a mouse:* these probably sounded charming the first time they were used, but they have since lost their appeal, and now sound tired and worn out.

Re-write using an original comparison:

Quiet as a mouse…

Now try these:

His heart was as hard as…

They were as friendly as…

She jumped like…

The wind blew like…

Write a direct comparison, without using "like" or "as."

Bahá'í administration is…

There are many other ways to increase the power of your words.
The exercises on this worksheet will give you a good start.

WORKSHOP # 8: Microphones and Media

REVIEW

a. Ways to add impact to a speech?
b. Why avoid apologies? Jargon? Abbreviations? Wordiness?

SHARE HOMEWORK: Two-minute speech on any topic

Positive critique notes on my talk:

Areas for improvement:

USING A MICROPHONE

☐ Where to position the mike in front of the audience
☐ How to adjust the height and angle of the mike
☐ How to turn the mike on and off
☐ How to remove and replace the mike in its holder
☐ How close to stand
☐ How to avoid tripping on the cord
☐ How to reduce feedback and adjust the volume
☐ Self introduction

Wrong amplifier placement   Correct amplifier placement

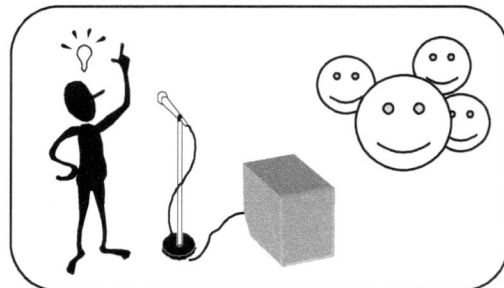

✳ Guidelines for Media Interviews

The Bahá'í community should carefully select the individual(s) who will represent the Faith to the media. Representatives should be knowledgeable, well-spoken, mature, dependable and with a dignified appearance.

(1) If you have an opportunity to prepare beforehand, study the topic of the interview and listen to the program a few times (or read the column) so you are familiar with the reporter's style and the pace of the show.

(2) Be prepared with a few statistics. Reporters often ask how many Bahá'ís there are in your town, the country and the world. Do not exaggerate.

(3) Dress modestly. Avoid stripes and red or white outfits for television as they look blurred on camera.

(4) Learn the interviewer's name and use it. If possible, chat with the reporter beforehand to break the ice.

(5) Be natural and sincere. Don't sound like you are reading a script.

(6) Listen to the questions carefully and respond briefly and accurately. Avoid one-word answers. They aren't very interesting and don't give the reporter much to work with. Also avoid lengthy explanations, which will probably be cut out. Chances are, your 15-minute session will be edited down to a 30-second sound bite. If you use a quote, keep it short.

(7) Don't use a lot of Bahá'í terms (Manifestation, dispensation, progressive revelation) or abbreviations (LSA, UHJ). The audience will not understand them. Refer to "the Bahá'í Faith" rather than "the Faith."

(8) If you don't know the answer to a question, say: "I don't know, but I'll check on it and get back to you." Then do it.

(9) Remember that the purpose of the interview is to convey factual information to the public. An interview is not a fireside and the reporter is not a seeker. An over-zealous Bahá'í can damage the reputation of the Faith and our relationship with the media.

(10) If the reporter is hostile, respond in a positive, educational way. Don't get upset, defensive, or repeat negative words from the question in your answer. Simply state the Bahá'í belief. Be sure to get your own positive message across, no matter what you are asked.

INTERVIEW PRACTICE

Interview #1

- Medium:

- Format:

- Tone:

- Topic:

- Three questions:

  1.

  2.

  3.

Interview #2

- Medium:

- Format:

- Tone:

- Topic:

- Three questions:

  1.

  2.

  3.

Sample Interview

Good afternoon viewers. I'm Victor Deerslayer from TV Channel 19. We are here on the steps of the courthouse with live coverage of the "Smith vs. State" adoption trial. My guest is Jennifer Smith, wife of the couple that was just denied adoption of a child of another race. The Smiths are purple and the child is pink.

Question 1:	Mrs. Smith, how do you feel about the verdict?
Question 2:	Why would a **purple** family want to adopt a **pink** child?
Question 3:	Did your religious faith play any part in your decision?
Audience:	Why should a child suffer just so you can prove your point?

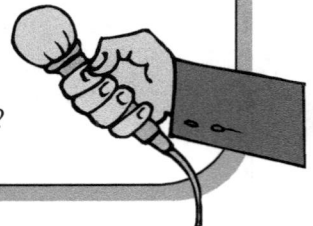

7. HOMEWORK: Read "The Vision of Race Unity" or other document chosen by your class. Using the worksheet, identify the title, author and date; determine the audience; give a brief summary with key points; select a quote from the document; and prepare a visual aid.

HOMEWORK

Title: _____

Author: _____ Publication Date: _____

Intended Audience: _____

Summary with key points:

Quote:

☐ Remember to bring a visual aid

WORKSHOP # 9: Official Presentations

REVIEW

a. Using a microphone:
b. Guidelines for media interviews:
c. A challenge and an opportunity:

SHARE HOMEWORK: "Vision of Race Unity" summary

PRESENTATION TO LOCAL OFFICIALS

Sample Presentation

(Students line up facing the Mayor)

ELENA: Good morning Mayor Jones and Council members. My name is Elena. Our Bahá'í youth group would like to make a short presentation.

(Students introduce themselves one by one.
Then two students step forward with the Race Unity booklet.)

GUS: On behalf of the Bahá'í community of Springfield, we would like to present you with this booklet, "The Vision of Race Unity."

(Show booklet.)

MINA: It talks about the elimination of racial prejudice and how we can establish unity between people of all colors and backgrounds.

GUS: Ming Li drew this picture to show what race unity means to her. And Jordan would like to share an excerpt from the booklet.

(Ming Li holds up her picture. Then Jordan steps forward,
recites a short memorized passage, and steps back.)

MINA: This booklet was written by the National Spiritual Assembly of the Bahá'ís of the United States, and it is being presented to leaders of thought around the country. We hope you enjoy reading it.

(Gus presents booklet to Mayor.)

☐ Practice making a formal presentation

SPEAKING THROUGH AN INTERPRETER

a. Do not speak louder than usual. The audience is not hard of hearing.
b. Look directly at the group or individual you are speaking to, not at the translator.
c. Speak slowly and clearly, using short sentences.
d. Stop after every sentence to allow for the translation.
e. Pay attention to your tone of voice. People will relate to your voice even if they do not understand the words.
f. Remember that the presentation will take twice the amount of time.

☐ Practice speaking through an interpreter

CLOSING ACTIVITIES ✔

☐ Tips for Public Speakers

☐ Self-Assessment

☐ Course Evaluation

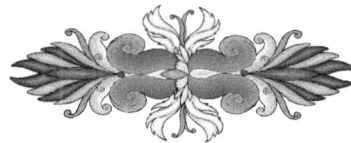

Congratulations!

You have completed the Public Speaking Course.

© UnityWorks LLC, Bahá'í Public Speaking, p.95

TIPS FOR PUBLIC SPEAKERS

✓ **PREPARATION**

A. Know your subject and prepare well beforehand. Study the talks of 'Abdu'l-Bahá for examples of a good speech.

B. Learn as much as you can about your audience and plan your talk around their needs. For example, if speaking to a group of teachers, you might address current educational concerns.

C. A speech can be memorized, but if you are nervous, a memorized talk can suddenly be forgotten. It is usually better to use keywords or pictures to remind you of the main points, rather than a script with the exact wording. Ask God to inspire you with the right words at the time.

D. One way to prepare notes for a talk is with a 3x5 card system. By using one keyword or picture on each card, you can easily add, delete or re-arrange topics as necessary. Number the cards and don't show them to the audience. As you become more experienced, you might put all of your points on the same card.

E. If you are using a script, you can <u>underline</u> key words for emphasis and mark pauses with a double line (//). Use a yellow highlighter on difficult words and practice them separately. Write out the phonetic pronunciation if necessary. You can also invent your own symbols to remind you to speed up, slow down, add a sound effect, recite a quote, show a visual aid, etc.

F. Keep it simple. Your speech should focus on one main topic with a few supporting points.

G. If appropriate, you can include music, poetry, drama, short quotations, analogies, stories, questions, sensory details, repetition, alliteration, visual aids, gestures, sound effects or other techniques for a more interesting presentation. Even silence can be used for dramatic effect. A well-timed pause can heighten the audience's curiosity. But don't overdo it! One or two of these techniques should be sufficient for a brief talk.

H. Engage the audience with memorable opening and closing lines.

I. Ask for help with the meaning and pronunciation of difficult words. There are several Bahá'í dictionaries and glossaries available to assist with this.

J. Practice the speech several times in front of a mirror and with your partner. You can also record it and play it back, listening for ways to improve.

K. Time your speech so you know how long it takes.

L. Consider arranging for a brief musical presentation before your speech. "Music," says 'Abdu'l-Bahá, "...has a great effect upon the human spirit....If a person desires to deliver a discourse, it will prove more effectual after musical melodies." (Compilation on Music, p. 77)

M. Arrive early to check arrangements in advance (microphone, audio player, projector, easel) and to get the "feel" of the room.

✓ PRESENTATION

N. Be well-groomed and appropriately dressed. This will make a good first impression.

O. Be natural and sincere. Don't sound like you are reading a script.

P. Never read a speech unless absolutely necessary, for example, if for legal reasons the entire text must be approved beforehand, or if the timing must be exact as in a radio commercial.

Q. Develop a connection with your audience. Begin with a greeting and imagine that you are talking to one or two individuals, not a faceless mass. Make eye contact with people around the room.

R. Speak with a strong voice so that the person in the back of the room can hear you.

S. Pronounce each word clearly without chopping off the endings.

T. Speak at a moderate speed without rushing. A slight pause at the end of key phrases, and after each sentence and paragraph, will make the speech easier to understand and ensure that the words don't all run together.

U. Speak with conviction and enthusiasm, using a melodious voice rather than a monotone.

V. Minimize the use of fill words such as *and, um, well, like* and *you know*.

W. Don't apologize for your speech or your speaking ability.

X. Avoid jargon and abbreviations. If you must use a specialized word, explain it.

Y. Be aware of your posture and body movements. Hands should be relaxed, either at your sides, gesturing, holding the microphone or on the podium.

Z. Keep your sense of humor.

✓ POST SCRIPT

Don't feel discouraged if your talk doesn't go exactly as planned or if the audience doesn't respond as you had hoped. You are only an instrument. The rest is between the listener and God. 'Abdu'l-Bahá explained this when He said, "The words I speak to you here tonight may produce no effect whatever. Some hearts may be affected, then soon forget; others owing to superstitious ideas...may even fail to hear and understand; but the blessed souls who are attentive...listening with the ear of acceptance, allowing my words to penetrate effectively, will advance day by day." *('Abdu'l-Bahá: Promulgation of Universal Peace, p. 149)*

> *"Heed not your weaknesses and frailty;*
> *fix your gaze upon the invincible power of the Lord...*
> *Arise in His name, put your trust wholly in Him,*
> *and be assured of ultimate victory."*
>
> **(The Báb: Dawn-Breakers, p. 94)**

PEER EVALUATION FORM

Speaker's Name: _____ Topic: _____

Main Points:

1.

2.

3.

After listening to this speech, I...

I especially liked:

You might try:

--✂--

PEER EVALUATION FORM

Speaker's Name: _____ Topic: _____

Main Points:

1.

2.

3.

After listening to this speech, I...

I especially liked:

You might try:

Public Speaking Workshop
COURSE EVALUATION

> Please answer the following questions and drop your completed form in the box. Your honest responses will help us to improve future courses. Thank you!

PLEASE RATE THE FOLLOWING: EXCELLENT POOR

- Physical facility 5 4 3 2 1
- Location 5 4 3 2 1
- Meeting times 5 4 3 2 1
- Course content 5 4 3 2 1
- Achievement of course objectives 5 4 3 2 1
- Instructor's preparation and organization 5 4 3 2 1
- Teaching style 5 4 3 2 1
- Handouts 5 4 3 2 1
- Benefit to you 5 4 3 2 1
- Benefit to your Bahá'í community 5 4 3 2 1

What did you like most about this course? _____

_____

What did you like least about this course? _____

_____

Suggestions for improvement or other comments? _____

_____

_____

Bahá'í Public Speaking

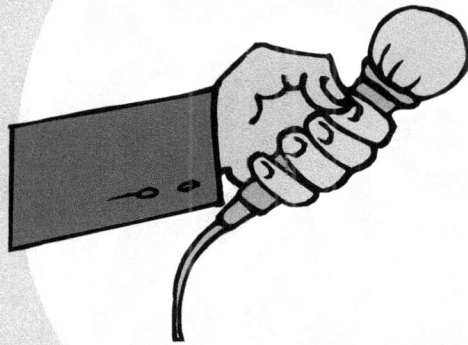

Certificate of Completion

Awarded to

_____

Teacher	Location	Date

© UnityWorks LLC, Bahá'í Public Speaking, p.101

Bahá'í Public Speaking

APPENDICES

A. Quotations on Speech

B. Help with Reading

C. Memorization Techniques

D. Keeping Time & Counting Fill Words

E. Approaching the Media

F. Responding to Controversy

G. Sample Letter of Introduction

H. Additional Projects

APPENDIX A

QUOTATIONS ON SPEECH

From the Bahá'í Writings

(1) "Unloose your tongues, and proclaim unceasingly His Cause. This shall be better for you than all the treasures of the past and of the future." *(Bahá'u'lláh: Gleanings, page 330)*

(2) "We have ordained that complete victory should be achieved through speech and utterance." *(Bahá'u'lláh: Tablets of Bahá'u'lláh, p. 197-198)*

(3) "Now is the time to speak forth and to deliver speeches, the time to teach and to give testimony. Loosen thy tongue...The Holy Spirit speaketh through the innermost essence of the human tongue..." *('Abdu'l-Bahá: Compilation on Women, p. 398)*

(4) "It is my earnest hope that you...may be so enkindled by the flame set ablaze by the hand of God as to illumine the whole world through the quickening energy of the love of God, and that through the eloquence of your speech, the fluency of your tongue, and the confirmations of the Holy Spirit you will be empowered to expound divine wisdom in such manner that men of eloquence, and the scholars and sages of the world, will be lost in bewilderment." *(Shoghi Effendi: Bahiyyih Khanum, p. 100)*

(5) "God willing, in a short time, women will become the same as men; they will take a leading position amongst the learned, will each have a fluent tongue and eloquent speech, and shine like unto lamps of guidance throughout the world." *('Abdu'l-Bahá: Compilation on Women, p. 397)*

(6) "Then, so much as capacity and capability allow, ye needs must deck the tree of being with fruits such as knowledge, wisdom, spiritual perception and eloquent speech." *(Bahá'u'lláh: Bahá'í Education - A Compilation, p. 5)*

(7) "Yea, certain persons shall in this divine dispensation produce heavenly children and such children shall promulgate the teachings of the Beauty of Abhá and serve His great Cause." *(Tablets of 'Abdu'l-Bahá, vol. 3, p. 647-8)*

(8) "It is the hope of 'Abdu'l-Bahá that those youthful souls...even as a nightingale endowed with speech, will cry out the secrets of the Heavenly Realm." *('Abdu'l-Bahá: Selections from the Writings of 'Abdu'l-Bahá, p. 134)*

(9) "Encourage ye the school children, from their earliest years, to deliver speeches of high quality, so that in their leisure time they will engage in giving cogent and effective talks, expressing themselves with clarity and eloquence." *('Abdu'l-Bahá: Selections from the Writings of 'Abdu'l-Bahá, p. 134)*

(10) "Even though children's activities have been a part of past Plans, these have fallen short of the need....Children are the most precious treasure a community can possess, for in them are the promise and guarantee of the future... Among the young ones in the community are those known as junior youth, who fall between the ages of, say, 12 and 15. They represent a special group with special needs... Creative attention must be devoted to involving them in programmes of activity that will engage their interests, mold their capacities for teaching and service...Against [the] gloomy backdrop of a decadent society, Bahá'í children should shine as the emblems of a better future." *(The Universal House of Justice: Ridván 2000 Message)*

(11) "The sanctified souls should ponder and meditate in their hearts regarding the methods of teaching. From the texts of the wondrous, heavenly Scriptures they should memorize phrases and passages bearing on various instances, so that in the course of their speech they may recite divine verses whenever the occasion demandeth it, inasmuch as these holy verses are the most potent elixir, the greatest and mightiest talisman. So potent is their influence that the hearer will have no cause for vacillation." *(Bahá'u'lláh: Tablets of Bahá'u'lláh, p. 200)*

(12) "Let them, at the very outset, teach their own selves, that their speech may attract the hearts of their hearers." *(Bahá'u'lláh quoted by Shoghi Effendi: Advent of Divine Justice, p.60)*

(13) "Grant, O my God, that I may not be reckoned among those whose ears are deaf, whose eyes are blind, whose tongues are speechless and whose hearts have failed to comprehend." *(The Báb: Selections from the Writings of The Báb, p. 216)*

(14) "In one of His Tablets, when reiterating the prohibition of the use of pulpits in any location, 'Abdu'l-Bahá has stressed that when Bahá'ís deliver their speeches in gatherings, they are to do so in an attitude of utmost humility and self-abnegation." *(Bahá'u'lláh: Kitab-i-Aqdas: Notes, p. 236)*

(15) "With hearts overflowing with the love of God, with souls gladdened by the heavenly glad-tidings, and with extreme humility and lowliness, let them speak out with eloquent speech, and praise and glorify the Great Lord, for they are the manifestations of His bounty and adorned with the crown of splendour." *('Abdu'l-Bahá: Compilation on Women, p. 396-7)*

(16) "O thou maid-servant of God! Whenever thou art intending to deliver a speech, turn thy face toward the Kingdom of ABHA and, with a heart detached, begin to talk. The breaths of the Holy Spirit will assist thee." *(Tablets of 'Abdu'l-Bahá, vol. 2, 1930 printing, p. 246)*

(17) "Blessed, blessed are ye for ye have arranged spiritual meetings and engaged in propounding divine proofs and evidences. Ye are intent on vindicating truth in support of the manifest Light of the Cause, through conclusive arguments and proofs based on the sacred scriptures of the past. This is a very noble aim, and this cherished hope a cause of the illumination of all peoples and nations." *('Abdu'l-Bahá: Compilation on Women, p. 397)*

(18) "As regards your teaching work: the Guardian has already advised you to stress in your talks the idea of a world superstate, and the concept of the Oneness of Mankind underlying it. In addition, he wishes you also to emphasize the fact that humanity, taken as a whole, has entered the most critical and momentous stage of its evolution, the stage of maturity. This idea of the coming of age of mankind constitutes the central core of the Bahá'í Teachings, and is the most distinguishing feature of the Revelation of Bahá'u'lláh." *(On behalf of Shoghi Effendi: Compilation of Compilations, vol. II, p. 194)*

(19) "An unprecedented, a carefully conceived, efficiently coordinated, nation-wide campaign, aiming at the proclamation of the Message of Bahá'u'lláh, through speeches, articles in the press, and radio broadcasts, should be promptly initiated and vigorously prosecuted. The universality of the Faith, its aims and purposes, episodes in its dramatic history, testimonials to its transforming power, and the character and distinguishing features of its World Order should be emphasized and explained to the general public, and particularly to eminent friends and leaders sympathetic to its cause..." *(Shoghi Effendi: Messages to America, p. 62)*

APPENDIX B

HELP WITH READING

When speaking in public or at Bahá'í gatherings, our students will have many opportunities to read aloud. Prayers and passages from the Bahá'í Writings are the revealed Word of God. They possess a special power and influence, and deserve to be read well. Our students should learn to read with fluency and reverence in order to capture more fully the spirit and beauty of the sacred Word. By learning effective techniques for tutoring reading, the teacher will also be able to provide this service in other settings.

The following suggestions are designed to assist those who wish to improve their reading skill and comprehension. Students should speak the language of instruction and have a basic knowledge of letters and sounds.

Assign a tutor to each student who needs assistance. They should arrange to meet (in person or by phone) on a regular basis for approximately 45 minutes each time. More frequent meetings (even daily) will produce faster results.

For the Tutor

The student will need several short books or pamphlets on topics of interest. Try out reading material at different levels of difficulty to find out where the student feels comfortable. The public library should be able to assist with this. There are also several Bahá'í magazines and a good selection of children's books available.

Select something just above the student's reading level so there is some challenge. While the student listens, you should read the entire book or selection (about five minutes' worth) using a normal speaking voice. Ask the student for a brief summary to insure comprehension. Then read only the first paragraph or section out loud while the student follows along on the page. Next, have the student read the paragraph once silently. Repeat this cycle until the student feels ready to read the paragraph out loud fluently, in a normal conversational voice. Have the student read the passage out loud. If you both agree that it was read well, proceed to the next paragraph. If not, repeat the process until the student is ready to read the passage aloud perfectly. Then go on to the next paragraph, until the book or selection is completed. You can check for comprehension by occasionally having students give a brief summary. Work for about thirty minutes at a time.

Teacher reads book; student listens	Teacher reads passage; student follows	Student reads same passage silently	Student reads passage aloud to teacher

You can work with several students at once if each student has an audio player with headphones. Make an audio recording of each book. Then follow the same tutoring method outlined above, with students listening to your voice on the recording. They can replay the recording to hear the paragraph again, and should inform you when they are ready to read out loud.

When reading, students should not point at words, track sentences with their fingers, or cover the text with frames or rulers. This prevents the eye from taking in larger quantities of print. It also prevents students from glancing ahead for context clues and slows them down. For the same reason, they should not move their lips while reading silently.

Leave about ten minutes at the end of every tutoring session for new reading. Have each student choose a new book at their current reading level, and read aloud one paragraph at a time. If students get stuck on a word, do not have them sound it out phonetically. If they could, they would have done so already. (Also, many words have the same spellings but are quite irregular in their pronunciation, e.g., try sounding out the "ea" in *heal, bread, break, reality, bear, earth, heart, theater and beauty.*) Instead, respond with the following strategy:

1. Ask the student to figure out the word using context clues. This means skipping over the word, reading to the next punctuation mark, then re-reading the sentence to determine the meaning.

2. If this doesn't work, give the student a hint such as the definition of the word, a synonym or a fill-in-the-blank sentence.

3. If the student is still stuck, tell him the word and its meaning.

4. Always have the student re-read the sentence.

When students are able to read at this level with minimal repetition on their main selection and almost no errors on their new reading, they are ready to advance to the next level. Your students might also enjoy some take-home reading at an easier level. You can provide them with appropriate material and should spend a few minutes at the beginning of the next session discussing it with them.

You might find it useful to make an audio recording of each student reading on the first and last days of your tutoring program in order to measure progress. Good luck!

Note: Ideas for this section were taken from experience with the ReadRight program and from several websites including: ReadRight.com, http://ToRead.com, ReadingRecovery.org, ReadingExchange.com, EduPlace.com, www.ed.gov/insts/americareads and ncrel.org/sdrs/timely/britoc.htm.

MEMORIZATION TECHNIQUES

Bahá'u'lláh tell His followers to "memorize phrases and passages" from the heavenly scriptures "so that in the course of their speech they may recite divine verses whenever the occasion demandeth it…" *(Tablets of Bahá'u'lláh, p. 200)*

Memorization is done by linking information: fitting new ideas into existing mental frameworks. A variety of techniques have been developed to help us recall information more easily. A few basic strategies are described below.

Simple Repetition

Read the passage out loud from start to finish. Repeat until it is memorized. Students can work alone, in pairs, or in groups, repeating after the teacher. Another method is to make an audio recording of the passage and replay it until it is learned.

Forward Buildup

Start at the beginning and recite the first phrase. Repeat until it is memorized, then add the second phrase. Continue in this manner until you have reached the end. Break a long selection into smaller parts and learn each part separately. Then connect them.

Backward Buildup

Start at the end and recite the last few words. Repeat until they are memorized. Then add the previous phrase and read through to the end. Continue in this manner until you have reached the beginning and have learned the entire passage.

Disappearing Act

Write a passage on the board and have students read it aloud several times. Then, using an eraser, swipe a diagonal path through the entire passage. This will leave a blank space on each line. Ask for student volunteers to read the passage again. Let everyone take a turn. Then make another eraser swipe and ask for another round of volunteers. Continue until the passage has completely disappeared.

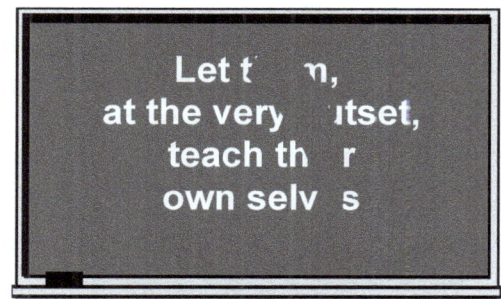

Let t   n,
at the very   itset,
teach th   r
own selv s

Acronyms

An acronym is a word formed by combining the first letters of a series of words, for example, SCUBA (Self Contained Underwater Breathing Apparatus). Acronyms are useful for remembering a group of words or topics in a particular order.

Rhymes and Melodies

Music is a powerful aid to memory. Many of us learned the letters of the alphabet to the tune of "Twinkle, Twinkle Little Star." Prayers and passages may be easier to remember if set to music.

Logical Patterns

Some material can be organized into a logical pattern to make memorization easier, for example, from small to large, simple to complex, old to new, and chronological order.

Visualization

Words can be tied to visual cues to aid recall. One method of visualization is called "chaining," where each image is used to suggest the next item on the list. If you are memorizing the prayer "Blessed is the Spot," you might create a string of mental images beginning with a dark circular spot on the front wall of a house. The house is then imagined in a beautiful garden "place" which happens to be in the center of a city. The city is laid out in the shape of a large heart, etc. As an aid to visualization, younger students can create drawings or cut and paste pictures on top of the written words.

Journey

This is another form of visualization. Imagine yourself walking along a familiar path, perhaps from your bedroom to the kitchen, or from your classroom to the cafeteria. Identify a number of landmarks along the way, for example, a certain tree, a bench, a flower garden. Use the path to remember your material by associating each landmark with one item you wish to recall. If you are trying to memorize a list of people, you might visualize the first person climbing the tree, the second person sitting on the bench, and the third person weeding the flower garden. See each person in your mind as you "walk" along the path. The more unusual the image, the easier it will be to remember. Use exaggeration, humor, silly movements or vivid pictures to spice up your journey. For example, the first person might be cutting down the tree; the second person, balancing the bench on her nose; and the third person, growing like a flower in the garden.

Memory Maps

This is another technique that uses visualization and association. The items to be recalled are mentally plugged into a familiar pattern such as a car or a human face. With a face, use the eyes to remind you of the first topic, the ears for the second and the mouth for the third. For example, if your talk is on race relations, the eyes could remind you to share the analogy of the "pupil of the eye."

Mnemonic Devices

Pronounced "new-MON-ic," this is a memory trick that helps you remember something difficult by associating it with a phrase that is easier to remember. For example, many schoolchildren have learned the lines of the treble clef in music by associating them with the phrase: "Every Good Boy Does Fine."

For additional ideas, visit: < www.geosoc.org/schools/pass/memory/memindex.htm >.

APPENDIX D

KEEPING TIME

Students should stick closely to the time allowed for each speech. This insures that the talk is long enough to be interesting and accomplish its purpose, while being short enough so as not to interfere with the rest of the program. It's all right to go a little over or under the limit, but as a courtesy to the next speaker, it is best to finish on time.

Before each timed speaking exercise, the teacher should appoint a timekeeper and provide a stopwatch or clock with a second hand. Ask the timekeeper to record the length of each speech, from the first to the last word. Use an apostrophe (') to indicate minutes, and a quotation mark (") to indicate seconds, as follows:

TIME
1-minute race unity speech

Elena	....	45"
Jamal	....	1'03"
LaTasha	....	48"
Jonathan	....	1'27"

After all the speeches have been given, ask for the timer's report. Example: "For the 1-minute race unity speech, Elena spoke for 45 seconds, Jamal for 1 minute and 3 seconds, etc." This brief report will provide useful feedback to each speaker.

COUNTING FILL WORDS

Students should try to minimize the use of distracting fill words (and, um, well, like, you know…) and use a pause instead. The teacher can appoint one person to monitor and record the use of fill words for each speech.

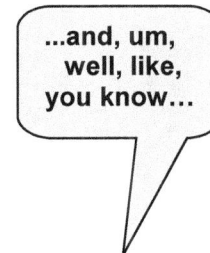

...and, um, well, like, you know...

FILL WORDS
2-minute fireside speech

Elena	.....//.....	2
Jamal	.....///.....	3
LaTasha	....	0
Jonathan	.THL.///..	8

When all the speeches are finished, the fill word counter can report. Example: "There were 13 fill words total. Elena had 2, Jamal had 3, LaTasha had 0, and Jonathan had 8."

APPROACHING THE MEDIA

The suggestions below are designed to assist your local Bahá'í community with its initial approach to the various media outlets in town. These exploratory visits to newspapers, radio and television stations may serve a variety of purposes, including:

- To introduce the Bahá'í community
- To ask about listing core activities in the community calendar
- To obtain information for an upcoming media campaign
- To offer an interesting person to be interviewed
- To present the Bahá'í perspective on a particular topic.
- To purchase time for a Bahá'í video.
- To propose a new community-service program such as a parenting series or a Spanish story hour

Always consult with the Bahá'í Institutions in your area before approaching the media.

Preparing for the Visit

1. Be familiar with the local media: read, watch and listen. Find out what types of programs are aired and what sections are included in the newspaper. Are there any public service announcements or a community calendar? Are there local talk shows? Who are the hosts? Does the paper allow guest editorials? What are the policies for letters to the editor?

2. Determine your media goals and objectives.

3. Set up an appointment with the editor, station manager or marketing director. Explain that you would like to meet with them on behalf of the Bahá'í community.

> Example: This is Loc Chu calling on behalf of the Bahá'ís of Our Town. I'd like to meet briefly with you to present some educational materials on the Bahá'í Faith and to obtain some information for a media campaign that we're planning. What would be a convenient day and time for you?

4. If going as a group, discuss the purpose of the visit, what to say and who will say it.

5. Prepare any materials needed for your visit and pray beforehand.

At the Station

1. Dress conservatively, arrive on time and be friendly to all.
2. Meet with the manager and explain the purpose of your visit.
3. Offer a press kit, photographs or other materials as appropriate.

4. If you are offering to produce a program or write a column, be specific about the topics you would like to address. You should also ask about their needs. What types of programs (educational, cultural, musical…) might the Bahá'ís provide as a service? If there is a talk show, what is the best way to contact the host about offering a Bahá'í guest?

5. If you are planning a media campaign, you might ask about:

- Audience size and characteristics
- Distribution area or signal coverage
- Hours of peak listenership or days of peak readership
- Policies on religious programming
- Usual rates for ads, spots and programs of different lengths
- Rates for different times of day or days of the week
- Rates for "run of schedule" (rotating time slots) or for specific programs
- Types of advertising packages and discounts for non-profit organizations
- Possibilities for free or low-cost advertising, e.g. community calendars, news releases, public service announcements (PSAs)
- Technical requirements, e.g. video format, exact PSA length, photograph quality, camera-ready ad sizes, etc.
- Submission deadlines

6. Ask if they would like to receive additional Bahá'í material for their files, and if so, what types of information would be useful.

After the Visit

1. Send a note to thank the manager for meeting with you.

2. Based on the information obtained, consult with the Bahá'í Institutions in your area to follow up on your plan.

> Approaching the media may seem intimidating to some, and futile to others - perhaps because the cost of advertising is so high and our funds and experience are so limited. However, we should not forget that all of these wondrous inventions were called into being by a Word from Bahá'u'lláh *(Gleanings, p. 141)* and should be used to promote His Cause.
>
> The members of one small Bahá'í community visited a local television station to inquire about the cost of a few 30-second spots—which was all they could afford. They left with a weekly half-hour community service program, sponsored by the Faith and paid for by the station. The program was on the air for over a year. In the words of the enthusiastic station manager, "Our town needs to hear this message!"
>
> *"As 'Abdu'l-Bahá said, nothing is impossible if we have faith."*
>
> Shoghi Effendi: *Dawn of a New Day*, p. 160

RESPONDING TO CONTROVERSY

The following ideas may prove useful in the event of public criticism or attacks on the Faith.

STEPS TO TAKE

1. Immediately inform the Local Spiritual Assembly of the situation.

2. The Assembly may wish to review any existing guidelines and policies, then consult with the Auxiliary Board and any media experts in the Bahá'í community.

3. Based on these consultations, a strategy will be devised.

BASIC PRINCIPLES

1. Designate only one spokesperson.

2. Respond quickly and accurately.

3. Don't say "no comment." It sounds like we have something to hide.

OTHER CONSIDERATIONS

1. A crisis is also an opportunity to talk about what we believe in, to develop links with the media, and to find supporters in the community.

2. If the media approaches you, direct them to the designated spokesperson. (Example: *"The one you really need to speak with about this is Dr. McMillan. Let me give you her number."*)

3. Respond in a positive, educational, non-adversarial way. (Example: *"Thank you for bringing that up. It gives me an opportunity to explain our perspective."*)

4. Don't be upset, defensive, or repeat negative words from the question in your answer. Be sure to get your own positive message across, no matter what you are asked.

5. Don't give unnecessary publicity to a negative incident. For example, don't barrage the newspaper with letters to the editor or call the press to issue a denial. Rather, wait until they contact you. Then decide whether and how best to respond. Many times, the situation will resolve on its own.

6. Each Bahá'í community should have a plan for responding to crisis situations.

SAMPLE LETTER OF INTRODUCTION

From the Bahá'í community to local officials, requesting a meeting for a formal presentation

---

Dear Mayor Standing Bear:

Warmest greetings from the Bahá'í Community of Worldview.

We take this opportunity to introduce ourselves and to offer you a copy of "The Vision of Race Unity," a statement by the National Spiritual Assembly of the Bahá'ís of the United States. This statement has been formally presented to leaders of thought throughout the country. We believe its message will be of great interest, and will lend support to our common efforts to foster understanding and harmonious relations among people of all races and ethnic backgrounds.

We have asked Dr. Errol Esteban to deliver "The Vision of Race Unity" on our behalf. He will be contacting you next week to arrange a convenient time. Any comments or questions you might have in response to this document will be warmly received.

Respectfully,

Ms. Sylvia Wong, Secretary
Spiritual Assembly of the Bahá'ís of Worldview

If this presentation is part of a larger campaign to reach particular populations, similar letters might be sent to those groups, for example: doctors, lawyers, teachers, government officials, university professors, community service clubs, student leadership associations, professional societies and others. Consider the following steps:

1. Select target groups.
2. Compile a mailing list for each group.
3. Obtain sufficient copies of the document to be presented.
4. Select and train the presentation teams (see Workshop #9).
5. Prepare and send the letters.
6. Call to arrange the appointments.
7. Make the presentations and schedule follow-up activities as needed.

> "National Spiritual Assemblies must promote wise and dignified approaches to people prominent in all areas of human endeavour, acquainting them with the nature of the Bahá'í community and the basic tenets of the Faith, and winning their esteem and friendship."
>
> *(Universal House of Justice to the Bahá'ís of the World, Naw-Rúz, 1979)*

ADDITIONAL PROJECTS

Personal Poster

When older students are working on preparing longer speeches, the younger children can create a personal poster or collage for presenting to the class. The poster should describe who they are: their goals, hobbies, family, pets, school, significant experiences, languages spoken, cultural traditions, favorite foods, etc. Provide craft materials (scissors, magazines, markers, construction paper, rulers, yarn, glue). When finished, give students one minute to explain their poster to the class. This is a good introductory activity for a new group.

Felt Lesson

Students can prepare a lesson suitable for presentation to a Bahá'í children's class, a fireside, a study circle, or any other small group. Felt can be used to make a visual aid for the talk. Felt is inexpensive, readily available at fabric stores, easy to manipulate and quick to clean up.

You will need scissors for each student, pieces of felt in a variety of colors, a felt display board (18" x 18" or larger), and two or three examples of existing felt lessons. These can be prepared by the teacher, or purchased commercially. (Bahá'í felt lessons and patterns for making them, can be found in the series of theme books for *Bahá'í Children's Classes and Retreats,* available from the Bahá'í Distribution Service: www.BahaiBookStore.com.) Pre-cut felt pieces (people, animals, geometric shapes, etc.) are available at many teacher supply stores. You will also need paper and pencils for sketching ideas.

Have students work alone or in pairs. Begin by demonstrating the sample felt lessons. Next have students demonstrate those same lessons. Then ask students to select their own topics, research them and prepare their lessons. Share when finished.

Youth Fireside

Some of the students in your class may wish to prepare a fireside for youth by youth. You can arrange a time for them to consult on the following:

1. Purpose of the fireside
2. Intended audience
3. Date, time and place for the event
4. Topic
5. Possible activities
6. Agenda and who will do what
7. Materials needed and who will bring them
8. Publicity
9. Refreshments

Here is the agenda for a fireside on Progressive ———➤
Revelation planned by the youth in our area:

- Welcome and introductions
- Short prayer
- Memorized quote on the topic
- Live music
- Talk on Progressive Revelation
- Skit of teachers in a school
- Summary
- Questions and answers
- More music
- Social time with refreshments

Seven Candles of Unity

This dramatic presentation is fun to do for a Feast or special event. Students will share 'Abdu'l-Bahá's prophecy about the seven candles of unity *(Selections from the Writings of 'Abdu'l-Bahá, p. 31-2)*, and will light a candle as each section is read aloud. Begin by dividing the passage into parts and selecting one reader for each part. Give each reader a copy of the entire passage with his or her part highlighted. Ask them to memorize it at home. Then rehearse together several times and practice lighting the candles. For the actual presentation, have students wear ethnic clothing representing different countries of the world. Remember to bring candles, candleholders and matches, along with printed copies of the passage to distribute to the audience. If possible, choose a room with lights on a dimmer switch so they can be turned down at the appropriate moment ("...the world's darkened horizon"). During the performance, sit in the front row with the script to prompt students in case they forget a line.

—See "The Power of Unity" Teacher's Guide (p. 120-121), available from Amazon and BDS, for a copy of the passage and detailed instructions for conducting this activity.

Monologues

Children can dress up to represent different figures from Bahá'í history such as Louis Gregory, Táhirih, or Dizzy Gillespie. (Avoid depicting the Central Figures of the Faith.) The teacher can prepare a monologue for each student to memorize, or older students can be given reference materials and a list of research questions, such as: Who was Táhirih? What was her childhood like? How did she find the Báb? Why is she important? Why did she dress up in a wedding gown when she knew she was going to be killed? How do you think she felt when she was being taken to her death? Performances should be in the first person, for example: "My name is Táhirih. When I was only a little girl..." Props (such as Táhirih's veil or a copy of the Koran) and appropriate background music (e.g. Persian chanting), can make the presentation more vivid.

—Idea from Jennifer Head of Kent, WA

Letters Home

Ask students to write a letter to their family from an important time and place in Bahá'í history. They might imagine, for example, that they are inside Fort Tabarsi, in the Black Pit with Bahá'u'lláh, or among the crowd at the martyrdom of the Báb. What did they see? Hear? Touch? Taste? Smell? How did they feel? Each student might choose a different event. Letters can then be edited and read aloud. Costumes and props can add to the scene.

—Idea from Jennifer Head of Kent, WA

Letters to God

Have children write a short letter to God, sharing their deepest thoughts and questions, for example: "Dear God: Why are there so many wars in the world? People are fighting about such silly things...." The letters can then be edited, memorized and shared in front of an audience.

— As performed by the New York City Bahá'í Children's Theater Company at the National Bahá'í Kingdom Conference in Milwaukee, June 2001

Famous Quotations

Children can memorize famous quotations to share. For example: "Hi. My name is Alex. I'm five years old. 'The earth is one country and mankind its citizens.' From the Bahá'í Writings." Quotations can be taken from Dr. Martin Luther King, Mahatma Gandhi, Mother Teresa, John F. Kennedy, Sojourner Truth, Sitting Bull, Chief Seattle or other well-known individual.

—See Appendix A in "Teaching Unity: A Guide for Parents and Teachers," available from Amazon and BDS, for an extensive compilation of suitable quotations on unity and diversity.

Still Life

Place a bunch of objects on a table and ask each student to pick one. Give them a few minutes to reflect on the object they have chosen, then have them deliver a short impromptu speech relating that item to the Bahá'í Faith in some way. For example, a book can be compared to the Holy Book of God, with many chapters, each representing a divine religion. A seed can be compared to the Kingdom of God on earth, since it begins as a tiny form, almost invisible under the ground, and grows slowly upward toward the light, until it becomes a great tree. A candle can be compared to a living martyr, weeping its life away drop by drop, in order to give its flame of light to the world.

— This is a difficult assignment, but can be a creative and enlightening experience for older students.

Note to teachers: If you would like to submit additional ideas for this section, please send them to the author for inclusion in any future editions of the manual. Submissions should be brief, clear and typed. Include your name, date and written permission to use your idea. Contributors will be acknowledged.

BIBLIOGRAPHY

Advent of Divine Justice. Shoghi Effendi. Bahá'í Publishing Trust: Wilmette, IL: 1990.

Bahá'í Children's Classes and Retreats. Randie Gottlieb. UnityWorks LLC: Yakima, Washington, 2004.

Bahá'í Education: A Compilation. Compiled by the Research Department of the Universal House of Justice. Bahá'í Publishing Trust: Wilmette, IL, 1977.

Bahá'í Prayers. Bahá'í Publishing Trust: Wilmette, IL, 1982.

Bahíyyih Khánum: The Greatest Holy Leaf. Compiled by the Research Department of the Universal House of Justice. World Centre Publications, Britain, 1982.

The Black Rose: A Story About 'Abdu'l-Bahá in America. Adapted for children by Anthony Lee. Kalimát Press: Los Angeles, CA, 1979.

Dawn of a New Day. Shoghi Effendi. Bahá'í Publishing Trust: New Delhi, India, 1970.

The Dawnbreakers. Translated and edited by Shoghi Effendi. Bahá'í Publishing Trust: Wilmette, IL, 1996.

Gleanings from the Writings of Bahá'u'lláh. Translated by Shoghi Effendi. Bahá'í Publishing Trust: Wilmette, IL, 1983.

God Passes By. Shoghi Effendi. Bahá'í Publishing Trust: Wilmette, IL, 1965.

The Hidden Words. Bahá'u'lláh. Bahá'í Publishing Trust: Wilmette, IL, 1994.

The Holy Bible. King James version. World Publishing Company: Cleveland, OH, 1959.

Kitáb-i-Aqdas. Bahá'u'lláh. Bahá'í Publishing Trust: Wilmette, IL, 1993.

Letter to the Continental Boards of Counsellors. International Teaching Centre. Bahá'í World Center: Haifa, Israel. 5 December 1988.

Lights of Guidance: A Bahá'í Reference File. Compiled by Helen Hornby. Bahá'í Publishing Trust: New Delhi, 1988.

Messages to America. Shoghi Effendi. Bahá'í Publishing Committee: Wilmette, 1947.

Messages to the Bahá'í World. Shoghi Effendi. Bahá'í Publishing Trust: Wilmette, IL, 1971.

Music, Compilation of Compilations, vol. II. Prepared by the Universal House of Justice. Bahá'í Publications Australia: Victoria, 1991.

Naw-Rúz 1979 Message to the Bahá'ís of the World. Universal House of Justice. Bahá'í World Center: Haifa, Israel, 1979.

Peace, Compilation of Compilations, Vol. II. Prepared by the Universal House of Justice. Bahá'í Publications Australia: Victoria, 1991.

Prayers and Meditations of Bahá'u'lláh: Translated by Shoghi Effendi. Bahá'í Publishing Trust: Wilmette, IL, 1969.

The Promise of World Peace. Universal House of Justice. Bahá'í Publishing Trust: Wilmette, IL, 1985.

Promulgation of Universal Peace: Talks Delivered by 'Abdu'l-Bahá. Compiled by Howard MacNutt. Bahá'í Publishing Trust: Wilmette, IL, 1982.

El Regalo. Cynthia Walcott. Bahá'í Publishing Trust: Wilmette, IL, 1976.

Ridván 2000 Message to the Bahá'ís of the World. Universal House of Justice. Bahá'í World Center: Haifa, Israel, 2000.

Selections from the Writings of 'Abdu'l-Bahá. Compiled by the Research Department of the Universal House of Justice. Bahá'í World Centre: Haifa, Israel, 1978.

Selections from the Writings of the Báb. Compiled by the Research Department of the Universal House of Justice. Bahá'í World Centre: Haifa, Israel, 1976.

"Sharing the Beauty of God" by Diedre Merrill and Gayle Woolson. *Brilliant Star Magazine.* Bahá'í Publishing Trust: Wilmette, IL, September-October 1983, p.31.

Tablets of 'Abdu'l-Bahá, Vols. II & III. Bahá'í Publishing Committee: New York, 1930.

Tablets of Bahá'u'lláh. Compiled by the Research Department of the Universal House of Justice. Bahá'í Publishing Trust: Wilmette, IL, 1988.

Two Wings of a Bird: The Equality of Women and Men. National Spiritual Assembly of the Bahá'ís of the United States. Bahá'í Publishing Trust, Wilmette, IL, 1997.

The Vision of Race Unity. National Spiritual Assembly of the Bahá'ís of the United States. Bahá'í Publishing Trust: Wilmette, IL, 1991.

Women, Compilation of Compilations, vol. II. Prepared by the Universal House of Justice. Bahá'í Publications Australia: Victoria, 1991.

WORKS BY THE SAME AUTHOR

Books are available from the U.S. Bahá'í Distribution Service:
www.BahaiBookStore.com, (800) 999-9019; and from Amazon.com.
PowerPoints and other downloads are available from: www.unityworksstore.com.

Teacher's Guides for Bahá'í Children's Classes and Retreats

These easy-to-use teacher's guides are filled with fun, hands-on, kid-tested learning activities designed for ages 8-12. A treasure trove of ideas for Bahá'í summer and winter schools, neighborhood classes, Holy Day programs, home schooling and weekend retreats.

The activities were developed and tested in the field, in response to the needs of teachers and children, and have been used successfully in multiple settings over many years. Lessons are organized in a sequential, step-by-step format, with each activity building on the previous one. The activities can also stand alone.

Each book focuses on a distinct theme, and comes complete with detailed lesson plans, copy-ready student handouts, patterns for making classroom materials, stories, songs, crafts, games, discussion starters, felt lessons, memory quotes, instructions for a children's performance and much more. The lessons are user-friendly and ready-to-go with very little outside preparation needed by the teacher.

These materials should not be seen as a replacement for the Ruhi curriculum utilized by the Training Institute, but teachers may find it useful to draw on them for supplementary activities.

What People Are Saying

- Such a valuable resource!
- Not just theory or good ideas.
- This retreat was life changing!
- All children's classes should be so enjoyable.
- Our children need and deserve this!
- You don't know how excited my kids are!!!
- My boys didn't want to leave.
- I loved the classes and I learned a lot.
- I loved every minute! Thank you! Thank you!
- Our summer camp was amazing and I did not
  have to reinvent the wheels of fun and education.
- My children had their best Bahá'í experience to date.
  Both in their opinion and mine.
- Fun, exciting and cool!

The Series Includes:

THEME 1: God and the Universe (210 pg)

- The Kingdoms of Creation
- God, the Creator
- Prayer, Our Connection with God
- What Is a Human Being?

THEME 2: The Manifestation of God (232 pg)

- The Station of the Manifestation
- Introduction to the Prophets
- Progressive Revelation
- One Common Faith

THEME 3: The Báb, Gate to Bahá'u'lláh (238 pg)

- The Báb: His Birth, Early Life and Station
- Declaration of the Báb
- Martyrdom of the Báb
- The Primal Point

THEME 4: Bahá'u'lláh, The Glory of God (159 pg)

- Bahá'u'lláh's Birth, Early Life and Station
- His Declaration
- His Exiles and Imprisonment
- Clouds of Glory

THEME 5: The Power of Unity (144 pg)

- The Power of Unity
- Unity in Diversity
- The Colors We Are
- Overcoming Prejudice

Your children will love to invite their friends!

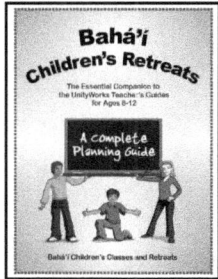

Bahá'í Children's Retreats: A Complete Planning Guide

Want to plan an unforgettable Bahá'í activity for children ages 8-12, but don't know where to begin? This practical guidebook covers planning, sponsorship, facility, publicity, materials, scheduling, registration, orientation, outdoor activities, meals, planning checklist and much more. Also included are medical release forms, recipes and a graduation certificate—everything you need to organize a successful children's retreat. Curriculum books on each theme available separately. **(68 pg softcover or download)**

Bahá'í Education

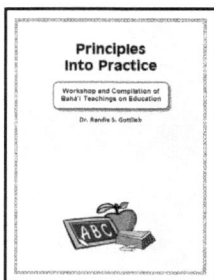

Principles Into Practice: Bahá'í Teachings on Education

This compilation of Bahá'í Writings is organized around 12 themes including: The Purpose and Goals of Education, The Curriculum, The Learning Environment and Discipline, Instructional Methods and Materials, Education for Service, and Educational Reform. Copy-ready handouts and detailed instructions are included for conducting an interactive workshop on the compilation. Suitable for educators who are friends of the Faith. **(46 pg download)**

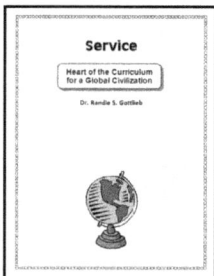

Service: Heart of the Curriculum for a Global Civilization

This monograph considers trends affecting teaching and learning, including the significance of service to mankind as a central organizing principle for our Bahá'í educational endeavors. It recommends practical strategies for systematically integrating service into the daily life and culture of our schools. **(15 pg download)**

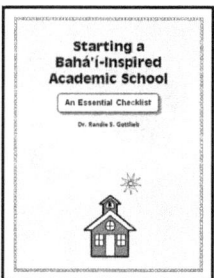

Starting a Bahá'í-Inspired Academic School

This booklet presents an essential checklist, basic guidelines and cautions for those considering the establishment of a Bahá'í-inspired academic school. It also provides a useful framework for organizing critical tasks and decisions including ownership, needs assessment, market analysis, legal matters, finances, facilities, equipment, personnel, scheduling, government requirements and academic matters. **(20 pg download)**

Escuela de las Naciones: A Bahá'í-Inspired Elementary School

The Escuela de las Naciones (School of the Nations) was established in the town of Arecibo, Puerto Rico in 1991, as a private, non-profit, competency-based, K-6 elementary school. This monograph provides an overview of the establishment and functioning of the school.
(15 pg download)

PowerPoint Firesides

This colorful PowerPoint series presents the basics of Bahá'í belief.

1. The Bahá'í Faith: An Introduction*
2. Central Figures of the Bahá'í Faith
3. The Proclamation of Bahá'u'lláh
4. The Power of Unity
5. Basic Principles of the Bahá'í Faith

----

* Available in English, Spanish and French

The Bahá'í Faith

What People Are Saying

- A great success tonight...excellent to use for youth.
- I don't know if the presentation could have gone any better!
- A wonderful introduction to the Teachings of the Faith and its history.
- A Bahá'í tour de force! A long-awaited and needed tool for the Cause!
- This was one of the most amazing teaching experiences I've ever had!
- The wrap-up of the semester—a perfect way to bring all the religions together.
- It was a response I think all Bahá'í youth alone in high school wish for.
- There wasn't even enough time to finish all of their questions!
- The experience was just amazing…The teacher asked us to return next year.
- We've got to get this out to the whole world.

Race Unity

Constructive Conversations on Race
Starter Kit with Guidelines and Activities

This easy-to-use conversation starter kit contains basic guidelines, a sequence of structured activities, and two colorful PowerPoint programs for facilitating a conversation about race with family, friends, classmates, co-workers, neighborhood and community groups. **(15 pg download)**

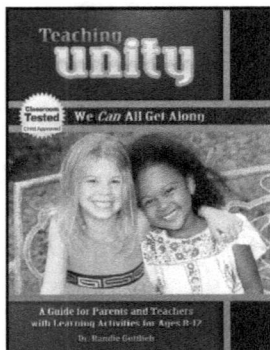

Constructive Conversations on Race
Conversation Starter Kit

Teaching Unity: We *Can* All Get Along
A Guide for Parents and Teachers with Learning Activities for Ages 8-12

Intended for the wider public, this easy-to-use curriculum guide has over 300 pages of hands-on learning activities for kids. It expands on "The Power of Unity" with dozens of new lessons and ideas. Ideal for academic classes, after-school clubs, Saturday or Sunday schools, scouting groups, holiday retreats and summer camps. **(306 pg softcover)**

See www.TeachingUnity.com for details.

More Teaching Tools

Once to Every Man and Nation (160 pages)
Stories About Becoming a Bahá'í

A great gift for seekers, this book brings together 37 heart-warming stories of how people became Bahá'ís. Read about the man who thought a fireside was a place to roast marshmallows, the woman who tried praying as an experiment, the minister's daughter who was terrified of death, the military veteran who was searching for an answer—and many more.

The contributors to *Once to Every Man and Nation* come from all over North America and represent a wide variety of cultural, racial, social and ethnic backgrounds. Young and old, black and white, each with a different experience of life, their very diversity demonstrates the universal appeal of the Bahá'í teachings.

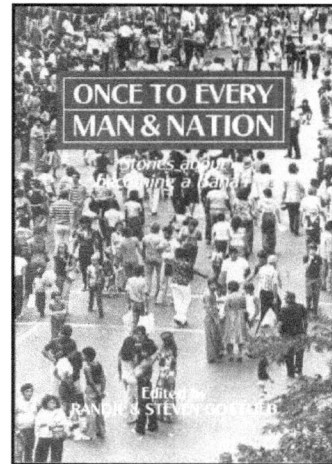

All welcome!
Study circles, devotional gatherings, children's classes & junior youth groups.

An invitation from the
Bahá'í Faith
(509) 999-1234
(800) 22-UNITE
www.bahai.org

Bahá'í Mini Ads
To complement our outreach and teaching efforts

These mini ads, each focused on a single topic, can be used in the newspaper as part of a local media campaign. The series includes basic Bahá'í beliefs and principles, short quotations from the Bahá'í Writings, offers of free literature, an invitation to the core activities, and an invitation to join the Bahá'í community. The file is in Microsoft Word format so it is easy to insert local contact information. **(Word and PDF download, 30 ads)**

The Five Year Plan

We are in the early stages of a vast evolutionary process leading to the establishment of a global civilization based on spiritual principles. Please visit our website for a variety of PowerPoints, workshops and study guides that provide an overview of the current Plan and its essential elements. **(PowerPoint and PDF downloads)**

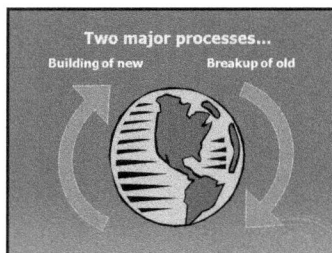

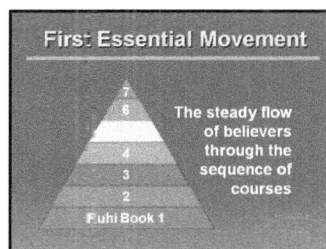

www.ingramcontent.com/pod-product-compliance
Lightning Source LLC
LaVergne TN
LVHW081317060426
835509LV00015B/1551